EBURY PRESS

POWER TO THE PARENT

Ishinna B. Sadana is a mother, parenting expert and trainer. It is her passion to work with parents and help them raise not only happier children but also become more optimistic in the process. She has a master's in human development and childhood studies as well as a PhD in human development.

Ishinna runs a centre called 'New Insights', where she has helped thousands of parents connect with their children through workshops and personal sessions. She believes that it's her life's purpose to enlighten the lives of parents—*Power to the Parent* is an important step towards fulfilling that goal. Ishinna aims to share her knowledge on a larger scale with many more parents who are searching for answers—she does this through social media, especially Instagram, where she has over a million followers.

POWER T THE PARENT

PARENTS WHO KNOW BETTER, DO BETTER

ISHINNA B. SADANA

EBURY
PRESS

An imprint of Penguin Random House

EBURY PRESS

Ebury Press is an imprint of the Penguin Random House group of companies
whose addresses can be found at global.penguinrandomhouse.com

Published by Penguin Random House India Pvt. Ltd
4th Floor, Capital Tower 1, MG Road,
Gurugram 122 002, Haryana, India

Penguin
Random House
India

First published in Ebury Press by Penguin Random House India 2024

Copyright © Ishinna B. Sadana 2024

10 9 8 7 6 5 4 3 2

ISBN 9780143465973

Typeset in Sabon by Manipal Technologies Limited, Manipal
Printed at Replika Press Pvt. Ltd, India

www.penguin.co.in

MIX
Paper from
responsible sources
FSC® C016779

To my children—Saiveer, who has taught me to become a better human being every day and helped me learn more than I could ever teach him, and Siraaj, who I carried in me for nine months while writing this book, and who gave me the strength and motivation to work on it.

To my family and my loved ones—without their support, this book wouldn't have been possible.

Contents

III: CALM PARENTING

IV: DISCIPLINE

V: CONSEQUENCES

VI: A FEW IMPORTANT PARENTING ISSUES

Introduction

'My child does not listen to me.'
'How can I handle my child's anger and tantrums?'
*'I am constantly losing my calm with my child and
I am unable to stop.'*
*'I don't want to get angry with my child, but I
don't know how else to get things done!'*
*'I am struggling every day with my child in
managing screen time/studies/feeding.'*
*'I want to be a gentle parent but I don't want my
child to become entitled or too pampered. Where
should I draw the line?'*

If any of these words resonate with you, then this is the
book for you!

Firstly, I want to congratulate you for choosing
to read this book, because that means you just took
the first step towards opening yourself up to knowing

better for your child and bringing a transformation in your parenting journey. Before you even start going through this book, I need you to know that no one, literally no one, can understand and connect with your child the way you can as a parent. Despite being a parenting expert, I cannot claim to know your children better than you do. In fact, when parents need guidance in their parenting journey, I depend on them for information about their children. After all, parents have known their children since the day they were born. They take care of them, love and nurture them, and go through so many experiences with them. I believe parents' love for their children is the most genuine love one can find in the world. Who can have better intentions for children than their own parents?

Becoming a parent is a beautiful experience, but we also know that it comes with its own set of challenges. These challenges become more difficult to overcome when we lack awareness about how children's brains develop, what their needs are, and how we can deal with and connect with them better.

We become parents as soon as our children are born, and oftentimes without any training or knowledge about raising them. For every job, we have training programmes, degrees and certificates, but for the most important job in this world, which is raising the next generation, we have no instruction manual. It is like setting up an electronic device like a speaker or a security camera at home without any instructions— we may try to connect the wires through trial and error, but it is more than likely that we will end up frustrated when things don't work out smoothly. An instruction manual or video would make the task much easier, right?

Now, imagine if we had knowledge about the latest science and research on how children's brains work and develop. If we knew why children behave the way they do, we could handle them better. If we also knew how our own behaviour can influence our children, we could use that knowledge to our advantage too. It would be so helpful to know how to manage our own emotions better while parenting our little ones. With this basic knowledge, we can become empowered in our journey as parents, and whenever we get stuck or face a crisis, we can find solutions to our problems on our own, instead of looking for advice from different sources which may or may not be authentic.

This is what I aim to do through this book: I want to help parents know better, widen their perspective and, thus, strengthen their intuition when it comes to their kids. When we merge true knowledge with our gut feeling, our parenting journey not only gets easier but also becomes more fulfilling.

In my own parenting journey, knowledge from the field of child development has helped me tremendously in understanding my child. That does not mean I do not face difficulties or make mistakes. What it does mean is that when I face a problem, I am able to sit back and assess the situation from an informed point of view and find better ways of dealing with the challenge. I am able to connect more effectively with my strong-willed child and can see his behaviour in a different light. I am also better able to understand and deal with my own emotions as a parent. I believe anyone can do this—we just need to have the right information.

I must also add that although my educational background provided me with knowledge about children early on, I was enlightened in many ways after I became a parent myself. When I practically used the development and parenting theories I read about with my child, I realized just how difficult it can be to be calm when faced with difficult parenting situations. I understood first-hand the mental and physical exhaustion a parent goes through, and the self-doubt and guilt we face in our journey. I also realized how difficult it can be to break our own patterns of thoughts and behaviours, and deal with our inner child. This is when my true insights into parenting came about and I could truly connect and empathize with other parents while guiding them in dealing with their children.

Coaching and connecting with thousands of parents, listening to their individual concerns and understanding their unique situations, widened my perspective and helped me identify the patterns that existed in different families. I could see why some of the parenting strategies do not work in practical situations, where the problems really lie and how we could solve them.

With my experience as a coach and a parent, I learnt ways to deal with the situations parents usually face in better and more effective ways—how to approach our children when they throw tantrums, when they refuse to cooperate or when we get stuck as parents. I understood how we can connect with our children and make our parenting journey beautiful in many ways. Every struggle I faced as a parent and every concern that another parent shared with me, became an opportunity for me to learn and evolve.

This book is my endeavour to share my knowledge with a larger number of parents. I do share information on social media and hold workshops to help and guide parents. While these are helpful in many ways, I believe that they are not enough to provide a complete picture as they cannot address all the doubts and questions parents have. With this book, my aim is to provide as many answers as possible and give as complete a picture as I can, to help parents—I want them to feel more empowered and confident by having all the tools and strategies they need to understand their children, and also deal with day-to-day challenges more effectively.

This book is designed not only to guide you with your children but also to help you know yourself better. If you keep an open mind, you will be able to pause and reflect on what you really want for your children and align your actions to your actual parenting goals. I have described many real-life examples in the book and shared my experiences so that you can gain practical insights that will guide you in different situations you may face with your children. Remember, every small change can lead to big changes and results. Although the book is intended to help parents of one to ten-year-old children, it is also applicable to any parent who is looking for insights into how to be calm in times of need and have a fulfilling relationship with their children.

Many times, I have heard parents say, 'I wish I knew this before.' It is time we equip ourselves with the right knowledge and be more informed so that we do not need to say these words any more. I suggest that as you read each chapter, process the information given and apply it in your parenting journey; and please be patient with yourself. Knowledge is the first step towards evolving, and I welcome you on this journey towards transforming yourself and your relationship with your child.

I

UNDERSTANDING
CHILDREN'S BEHAVIOUR

1

Why Do Children Behave the Way They Do?

A two-year-old boy was playing with a glass object, and afraid that the object might break, his mother took it away. The minute she did that, the boy started howling and banging his head on the wall. The mother got very anxious and tried to explain to the toddler that he would get hurt, but he kept crying louder and demanded the glass object back. The mother started to get irritated and began to shout at the child. This continued for a while before the boy settled down.

* * *

A four-year-old girl had been watching television for an hour. When her father told her to switch off the TV, she did not listen. He switched off the screen himself. At that, the girl started screaming and flung herself on the floor in a fit. Her father tried to reason with her that it was late and she had already watched enough TV, but she kept on crying until her father switched on the television for another ten minutes!

* * *

A seven-year-old boy was playing with his one-year-old sister. When his sister took one of his superhero figurines, the boy got extremely angry and hit her. When their mother scolded the boy and told him to not hit his sister, he started arguing and saying things such as, 'You always support her. You don't love me.' He cried for an hour before he calmed down.

What is going on with these children? Why are they behaving in such ways? Why can't they understand simple logic and not be so dramatic?

We assume that our children are behaving in these ways and being completely unreasonable in their reactions on purpose. We call these behaviours 'tantrums' and at times, they can be so frustrating to deal with that we tend to lose our patience. In response to the 'unreasonable' behaviour of our children, we become either too angry or too anxious.

One of the reasons we get so triggered is that we don't know how our children's brains work and why they behave the way they do. This lack of information makes us judge our children (*How can my child behave like this?*) or take their behaviour personally (*Why is my child doing this to me?*). As a result, we are unable to effectively engage with our children in such situations; our children's tantrums keep increasing and their outbursts become more and more unmanageable, making our parenting journey very stressful.

Let us understand the typical behaviours seen during tantrums.

In children, tantrums may include behaviour such as:

- crying
- screaming
- lying down on the floor
- throwing things
- hurting themselves
- getting angry or aggressive
- being stubborn
- being too clingy
- arguing and
- talking rudely.

These kinds of behaviour look very dramatic but the fact is that 'tantrums' are nothing but *emotions being expressed physically through the child's body as the child is unable to handle what he or she is feeling*. Emotions that cause such reactions may include frustration, disappointment, being upset, feeling anger and so on.

Feeling these emotions is a natural part of being human. If we think about it, we will realize that we all feel these emotions in our everyday lives when different situations lead us to feel disappointed, frustrated, sad and angry. And if we look back and consider moments when we feel like this, we become aware that such emotions do affect our behaviour. The way we behave and react to situations differs depending on how we are feeling at that moment.

Let us reflect on the following examples to understand this:

Situation 1: Imagine you are in your room and you just got off a call with your boss in which s/he blamed you for something and you are now very upset. Right then, your child enters the room and spills water on the floor. What will be your reaction?

Situation 2: You are in your room and receive a call from your boss in which s/he informs you that you have been promoted. S/he lavishly praises you for your effort at work and as the call ends, you feel extremely happy about the good news. Just then, your child enters the room and spills water on the floor. Do you think your reaction will be different from your reaction in Situation 1?

When we are stressed about something, we tend to lose our patience in circumstances where we otherwise would have been calmer. Depending on how we are feeling, our tone, gestures and the words we use are affected. This is because our feelings and behaviours are indeed connected!

Our behaviour is influenced by what we are feeling. Every behaviour is an outcome of an existing emotion at that moment unless we consciously regulate it.

Now let us reconsider our children's behaviours, which are also affected when they feel any emotion. It is important to understand that there is always an emotion hiding under a tantrum. What the child starts feeling may be 'frustration' when they are unable to stack the building blocks and thus they end up throwing their toys all over the floor; or there may be 'disappointment' because they lose a board game, which results in them crying and spoiling the game. It is very important to note here that though these instances may seem trivial to us adults, they are way more important for the child, and their feelings are very real.

The most important point to understand here is that there is a huge difference between an adult's brain and a child's brain. A child's brain is quite underdeveloped and is not yet capable of comprehending emotions and regulating them. Thus, children mostly express their emotions in their behaviour *as they are*—they can't help it as they do not yet have well-developed brains that can regulate how they feel and what they do. That is the reason children behave in significantly different ways from adults.

Adults are able to regulate their behaviour in different situations. This means that in spite of what they are feeling, adults can change their behaviour to suit the situation that they find themselves in. For example, when we have guests at home, we put a smile on our faces even when we are feeling extremely low about something. We don't start crying in front of them. We regulate our emotions and don't let them affect our behaviour for the duration that our guests are around.

Take another example: When we are at home and our child is not listening to us, we may end up shouting at them, but when we are in public—say at a mall—and our child refuses to listen to us, we consciously regulate our voice and words even if we are feeling angry because there are strangers around and we do not want to create a scene.

Adults are better able to filter and mould their reactions according to their circumstances in spite of the emotions they are feeling thanks to their fully developed brains. This ability is controlled by the part of the brain known as the prefrontal cortex, which sits right behind our forehead. In young children, the prefrontal cortex is still under construction and is not developed completely.

That is why a child's behaviour is very different from an adult's behaviour. It's simply because their brain is different!

Let me give you an example here.

When my son, Saiveer, was three years old, we were practising writing numbers on a whiteboard. He was really interested in numbers but was struggling to copy the right formations. At one point, when Saiveer couldn't copy the number '5' correctly, he got so frustrated that he wiped out the entire whiteboard aggressively and threw the duster at my face. I was taken aback because it was a very dramatic reaction and I could have gotten hurt. But at that moment, instead of overreacting, I said, 'OK! I think you got really angry, but we can't hit, sweetheart.' I paused for ten seconds and then asked him, 'Are you okay?' He got so overwhelmed that he said, 'I didn't want to do that mamma' and came into my arms. I just hugged him and said, 'I know'.

Saiveer experienced frustration and couldn't handle that emotion. His brain could not regulate his behaviour, and the emotion was expressed directly through his body and actions; as a result, he impulsively threw the duster at my face.

Despite understanding this, it was not easy for me to not react in the moment. I literally had to take a breath before I could respond calmly. But if I had gotten angry and blamed Saiveer for hurting me, the situation would have gotten worse. It would have made him even more dysregulated* and it would have escalated the tantrum. I will discuss in detail how to deal with children's tantrums in the following chapters.

So, based on what we have discussed here we can conclude that 'children's behaviour is guided by their feelings'. Now we can understand why a five-year-old

---

* The term used to describe people who are unable to control or regulate their emotional responses, which can lead to significant mood swings and changes.

starts shouting and howling when we take the screen away from them, even after they have watched it for an hour already. The child feels the emotions of anger and is unable to regulate it. It is worth noting here that a child who is very happy and excited may also tend to pull out their hair, hurt themselves or start screaming at the top of their voice. Children are often not able to regulate the feeling of excitement as well.

When we start seeing our children's behaviour in this light, we can make meaning of all the drama that we face around their tantrums. Children are quite literally struggling to handle their feelings when they cry, scream or are being rude. They don't enjoy behaving like this and suffer emotionally.

Imagine how you feel when you get angry and yell at your child.

Do you enjoy that moment? Or do you feel really bad, perhaps emotionally suffering yourself? And now think:

How would you want others to handle you when you are angry?

Would you not want someone to understand you?

Without judging you?

Without insulting you?

Without threatening you?

What we need when we are angry is what our children need when they are angry!

So, the next time when your child is throwing a tantrum, remind yourself, 'My child is feeling something that they are unable to understand and process and is vulnerable right now.' Children do not even know what emotions are. They are just experiencing their emotions in the form of vibrations coursing through their bodies that make them behave in a certain way. Believe me, they do not enjoy it. They may even be scared for a moment and need our help to make sense of what they are going through.

Take, for example, the following instance.

When Saiveer was six years old, he went to the market with his dad. By the time they came back home, Saiveer was very hungry. Though he could not understand it, he was clearly getting dysregulated due to the hunger he was feeling. At the same time, he wanted to show me his new shoes. As I wasn't sure if we might have to return the shoes later, I asked Saiveer to not take off the tags. But he couldn't control his hands and impulsively removed the tag. He then wanted to untie the laces but was struggling with them. He couldn't manage the frustration he was feeling and started crying loudly for a few seconds and then stopped. The minute I tried to help him wear the shoes, he told me, 'Pagal hai' (you are mad). Hunger had taken its hold over him and my son couldn't regulate what he was feeling. I chose not to discipline him at that moment, moved away from the situation and went to prepare his meal.

Here, Saiveer's behaviour was communicating to me that he was not feeling good and needed my help. Our children actually communicate to us that they need help through their so-called irrational behaviours. They are unable to use words when they are overwhelmed because they are not equipped to do so since their brain is still developing. But when we, the adults, lack information about how our children's brains work, we may think that they are being rude and are giving us a hard time.

It is time that we start seeing the reason behind our children's behaviour instead of judging them for it or taking it personally. There is always a feeling or emotion causing a difficult behaviour even though it is not visible to us. When we understand this, our perspective shifts from 'my child is being unreasonable and making the situation difficult' to 'my child is struggling to regulate his emotions and needs my help'. Only when we consciously remember this and get curious to learn more, can we explore and diagnose what is really causing our children to behave the way they are.

2

Dealing with Tantrums

The way in which we respond to our children's tantrums matters a lot. When we deal with these behaviours in the right way, tantrums become manageable and children also learn to handle their emotions better. But when we are unable to effectively deal with tantrums, we see that behaviour increasing in frequency and intensity.

There are three main steps to follow when a child throws a tantrum, but there are also some common mistakes that we make during a tantrum and need to be careful about. I am going to describe both in this chapter.

Three Steps to Deal with Tantrums

1. *The first step is to 'Be Calm'.*

No matter how clichéd this sounds, it is going to be the most helpful step during our children's tantrums.

It is normal to feel triggered when our child is crying uncontrollably, screaming at the top of their voice or arguing non-stop. After all, it is a very emotional situation and can intimidate us. It may make us lose control over our own behaviour and we may end up yelling and shouting ourselves because we want the tantrum to just stop.

Sometimes, when a tantrum occurs, parents do not get angry but anxious. They get so overwhelmed that though they may not yell, they are not calm either. They feel extremely uncomfortable looking at the child and are unable to respond effectively. They may even give in to their children's demands or compensate by giving them something else just to make the tantrum stop.

An angry or anxious parent cannot effectively deal with a child who is throwing a tantrum. Children look at us, their parents, as authority figures. After all, we are the ones taking care of them and forming the rules and boundaries for their behaviour. When we as authority figures lose control over ourselves and our children see us in that state, they feel unsafe and thus become even more dysregulated. This means that when we lose our calm, our child's tantrum escalates at that moment. It also means that the problematic behaviour will start to repeat more frequently in the future.

When we lose control over our behaviour, we become a part of the problem instead of solving it. In a way, we become a child along with our children. It is time for us parents to reflect on this: *Do I want to become a problem-solver or do I want to add to problematic situations around my child?*

The first step towards handling the situation is to calm ourselves down. We have to remind ourselves that we are adults and our child needs help in regulating their emotions. Though I do understand that it is not going to be easy to remain calm, especially when your child is continuously arguing with you and pushing your buttons, only when we are calm, can we think clearly, make better decisions and indulge in a more helpful response while helping our child deal with their emotions better.

So, next time you see your child throwing a tantrum, pause and take deep breaths (literally) before responding to your dysregulated child. When you pause, it gives you a few seconds to change your unhelpful response to a more helpful one.

And during that pause, watch what you are thinking and consciously try to change it—it is what we are thinking that is making us angry or anxious.

We mostly lose our calm during a tantrum when we are thinking something like this:

'Why is my child throwing a tantrum?'

'I do everything for my child and still I get this?'

'What will other people think of me? What kind of a parent I am?'

These thoughts will not help us in being calm; this is actually our mind telling us stories. The good news is, we can pause and change our thought. We can choose to think in the following ways:

'My child is feeling emotions that he/she can't handle. My child is suffering and needs my help. I need to stay calm to help him. Else, I will become part of the problem instead of solving it.'

You will realize that breathing and changing your thoughts will calm even your body. Observe how your body is behaving during your child's tantrums. If you are overreacting, then chances are that your body is tense and vibrating (just like your child's). Breathe and calm your body and mind.

When we do this, it drastically changes our response towards our child. We become kinder and more patient and thus, more helpful. Remember, this does not mean that we are giving in to our child's demands or being lenient. When we are calm, we are just being an adult instead of being another child in the situation.

In the following section dedicated to the topic, we will learn in detail about the benefits of being calm and how we can practise being calm.

2. *While being calm, empathize with your child's emotions.*

If a child is throwing a tantrum, there is a reason leading to that behaviour. The reason may not be that important to us or may even seem illogical. Nevertheless, it is something that is making the child upset. Let's take two examples to understand this.

a. *Your six-year-old has already had enough screen time but is refusing to switch the TV off. So you switch off the screen yourself. Your child gets very angry about it and starts arguing and complaining incessantly.*

b. *A father tells his three-year-old that he will take her for a five-minute ride in the car before he leaves for work. But he remembers that he has an urgent call and leaves instantly. The child gets very upset and starts howling while standing at the door with the mother.*

Our natural reaction in such a situation is to logically explain the situation to our children. We may try saying some of the following things when faced with the situations described above.

a. *'You have already watched the screen for too long. You told me you would turn it off now. You know it is not good for your eyes. We can only watch the screen for forty minutes a day—that is what we decided.'*
b. *'Papa had to leave because he had a meeting. He will take you for a drive in the evening. Stop crying now. Papa had to go to work.'*

We tend to repeat these lines over and over, trying to make our children understand the situation. But, when we go on continuously explaining in this way, the intensity of the tantrums starts increasing. This is because of two reasons.

First, an explanation is based on logic, which the child is unable to understand in the midst of a tantrum when they are overwhelmed with emotions. This happens because, during the tantrum, the child's emotional brain gets so activated that they are unable to access the logical brain. So, whatever explanations we try to give, they do not get through to the child. To help the child understand our logic, we first need to connect with their emotion.

Second, when we go on explaining something to the child, we engage in a tantrum and give this sort of behaviour a lot of undue attention. Not only does the child not understand the explanation, but they may also increase the intensity of the tantrum because they see that it is getting exclusive attention from the parent in the form of continuous interaction.

Therefore, during a tantrum, we need to stop providing repeated explanations to children and start empathizing with them instead. Children are looking for emotional connection and not logic to calm down.

In the two situations we are discussing, empathy looks like this:

a. *'I know you really wanted to complete the episode you were watching on the TV just now. Oh, I can see you are feeling bad about not finishing watching it. But we will watch the screen in the evening now.'*

b. *'Oh, you are upset because Papa left and didn't take you? That's what is bothering you. I can see that, sweetheart. I know. Papa will take you in the evening now.'*

Here, we are talking about what the child is going through and validating their emotions instead of repeating the same explanations that are clearly not having the desired effect of calming the child. When we are calm and empathize with them in this way, our children feel more understood and connected to us. Sometimes we don't even need to use many words to empathize and what's required is only to say '*I know*' to express that we understand what they are going through.

Important: Do not over-express empathy. We do not need to keep repeating lines of empathy just like we should not repeat explanations. Doing that will also end up escalating the tantrum because again it will give the child a lot of undue attention. Children need space to feel their feelings before they calm down. So, a couple of lines of empathy are enough. Then we need to pause and observe the child while we let empathy be palpable in our bodies and our expressions.

When we empathize with our children and validate what they are feeling, it helps them to access their logical brain and they are finally able to regulate themselves. They may even understand the logic and boundaries that we are trying to communicate to them.

Important: Empathy is not effective if it is not genuine. Make sure that you actually have empathy and that it is not something that you are using to merely solve the situation. If we do not genuinely feel the words we are saying, it becomes manipulation and that will not help the situation. Sometimes, we merely mouth commonly used sentences such as 'I understand you are feeling bad' without really meaning them when talking to our children. Trust me, children realize it when we do not mean what we say. So, remember that 'empathy is only effective if it is genuine!'

In fact, we can empathize even without words. Empathy needs to be in our body language, expressions and tone. You can just say 'I know'. Saying 'I know' is very effective when we do not want to use too many words. Even when children are too young and cannot connect with long sentences since their language skills are still developing, 'I know' works beautifully. It lets the child know that we are there and we understand. And our calm and regulated body does the job too.

Meltdowns: Sometimes children go through meltdowns or emotional outbursts, which are extreme forms of tantrums. Meltdowns happen when children get completely dysregulated and don't listen to even a word of what we are saying. It is often a hungry or overtired child who will experience meltdowns. In such situations, it is better to say nothing, radiate empathy from the body and expressions, and pause to let the child's emotions pass before doing anything else. Here, I want to share my own experience of a meltdown my son experienced.

Saiveer was two and a half at this time. He was so hungry one day that he got triggered by the fact that 'Mommy had put too much juice in one cup' and it became the starting point of the meltdown. He began to howl loudly and would not listen to anything. Whatever he said was completely illogical and I could see that he was struggling to regulate. All my worried family members started gathering around us, which triggered him further. I had to be proactive in the situation, so I picked him up and took him to my room to make him feel safe. I had to remember to keep breathing consciously as the whole situation was making me anxious. I regulated myself and kept saying 'I know' to Saiveer and let him cry and even scream for some time as there were a lot of emotions that he needed to let out before he could begin to calm down. I kept maintaining my calm (especially in my body), as that was the only thing that I could do to help him feel safe.

It took him almost twenty minutes before he finally came to me and I hugged him tight. The meltdown started ebbing at this point, I gave him something to eat and soon, he felt better.

Meltdowns are like an emotional storm. Imagine there is a real storm outside your house that forces you to cancel your plans. Will you open the window and start shouting at the storm, 'Why are you doing this?' Or will you wait for the storm to pass? Well, you have both options, but you will have to let the storm end in both cases. So, during a meltdown, we must just sit and empathize through our bodies and expressions and wait for the child's emotions to pass. During a meltdown, what a child really needs is a calm adult.

3. *Let the tantrum pass without giving in.*

Children take time to process feelings and release them from their bodies. Thus, we need to be patient and let the tantrum pass without giving in to the demand that led to the tantrum in the first place.

Sometimes parents complain, 'Even when I empathize, my child still continues to throw the tantrum.' Expect that to happen. We need to give children space to feel their feelings. So, after empathizing using a couple of sentences, pause and observe the child while maintaining your calm.

Also, during a tantrum, it is very important to allow some behaviours such as crying, screaming or lying down on the floor. Avoid saying such things as:

'Don't lie on the floor, it is dirty'
'Stop crying first; then I will talk'
'Why are you shouting like this?'

Such words do not help because children cannot instantly stop the commotion taking place in their bodies. They need to let out what they are feeling in some way. In fact, when we say such things, they sometimes result in that behaviour intensifying.

Of course, we do need to set boundaries when a child's behaviour is harmful to someone—for example, if a child starts hitting or throws something breakable. But even that boundary to stop the harmful behaviour must be set by us calmly and firmly without losing control.

Let me share with you how I put a boundary in place with Saiveer when he started hitting me during the meltdown I described earlier.

After I moved Saiveer to my room, at one point, he got so dysregulated that he started hitting me. I told *him, 'I know you are upset, but we can't hit, baccha.'** *Still, he hit me again. So, I got up and moved a little away as I couldn't let him hit me. I needed to help him regulate his behaviour.*

[Here, I will suggest that you do not hold your child's hands to stop them from hitting. When we do that, the child sees it as an attack and then they get more aggressive in order to defend themselves.]

I calmly stepped back when Saiveer came to hit me one more time and said, 'If you hit me again, I will go in the washroom.' He did hit me—that's when I went to the washroom, closed the door and counted to five to myself. He started banging on the washroom door (the room was completely safe for him). I opened the door after the count of five and said, 'Can I come out now? Will you be able to control your hands?'

Saiveer was about to hit me again, and so I started to close the door once more. But to my relief, he cried out, 'I will not hit, come out.' I came out that very instant and hugged him.

Here, my son was so dysregulated that I had to use the technique called 'facing consequences' to help him control his hands. I am going to discuss this technique in detail in the section titled 'Discipline' in the book. It is a beautiful technique to help children practise regulating their behaviour.

Coming back to our initial point about setting boundaries, I want to reinforce the point that we do need

---

* Kiddo.

to set them during a tantrum but only for behaviours that are harmful. We may not always have to take such extreme steps as described here in my son's example. Sometimes, when we allow children to express emotions through some behaviours that are not harmful and maintain our calm during the tantrum, they are able to control the actions we put boundaries around. We have to remember to be firm and not angry, but communicate the message that 'it is okay to feel what you are feeling, but you still can't hurt other people'.

FAQ

Should we not ignore our children's tantrums?

It is true that when we give undue attention to tantrums, their frequency tends to increase. But it is also true that when we completely ignore the tantrum, a child feels abandoned as they emotionally suffer during the tantrum and need our help.

So, we can find a balance in the following way: We approach the tantrum calmly, we empathize in a couple of sentences and after we have done our bit, we offer a hug to our child. Typically, if the child is very dysregulated, he or she will not accept the hug. Here, we stop paying attention to the tantrum and simply say: 'I can see you are struggling. I am here doing my work; you can come to me for a hug. I love you.' At this point, we stop paying attention but our tone still needs to be calm and we must let the child know that we are available. We have to make sure that we are not irritated. This is the way to not pay undue attention to the tantrum but not completely ignore it either.

Common Mistakes That Increase Tantrums

1. Over-empathizing

Empathy is a very effective tool but when we overdo it, instead of helping, it ends up increasing the intensity and frequency of tantrums. This happens because it seems to the child that the behaviour of tantrums gets a lot of attention. So, we need to remember to NOT over-empathize by repeating the words of empathy again and again in different ways. We do not even need to keep giving a response or engaging with the child in every moment of the tantrum. After empathizing in a few sentences, pause and stop speaking; let empathy stay in your body and expressions. If you think your child is looking at you, you can just say, 'I know' to fill the silence.

2. Explaining repeatedly

This is another mistake that most parents make, that is, explaining too much and literally repeating words. As we discussed earlier, children cannot understand logic at the time of the tantrum. Giving logical explanations repeatedly only seems like being given attention and nothing useful actually gets across to them. Instead, they end up feeling not understood and not being validated for their feelings because we are only focusing on the reasoning and not on their emotions.

Genuine empathy, not explanations, helps children feel connected and understood.

3. Giving in to the tantrum

When we give our children the thing they want and because of which the tantrum started, tantrums will undoubtedly reoccur more often in the future. Not only will they increase in frequency, but also the duration and intensity of the tantrums will increase.

Tantrums become *addictive behaviours* when children feel that they are helping them in getting what they want. For example, when we give them the screen that they wanted because they were crying too much, crying will definitely increase. It is important to stick to our decision firmly and respectfully while empathizing with the child at the same time. Being empathetic does not mean we are being lenient. We are only validating the child's feelings, but we are not giving in to their demand.

Important: There are times when we are in such a situation that we end up giving in to our child's tantrums. I can understand that completely. In such instances, I suggest that you observe such situations and be more mindful—if you know you will not be able to follow through with your 'no', then give your child what they want before the tantrum starts.

For this, you will have to pause and think before saying 'yes' or 'no' to your child in any situation. Remember, you are the parent and you can decide to say 'yes' if you think you need to.

But when we change our 'no' to 'yes' because of a tantrum, then firstly, children will stop taking our 'no' seriously and secondly, they will try using tantrums more often to change our decision.

4. Compensating to stop the tantrum

Sometimes, even though we don't give in to the demands of the tantrum, we offer something else to the child to make them stop the tantrum. For example, we say, 'Please stop crying like this. I don't have the ice cream but you can have the chocolate; just don't cry.'

Essentially, we do this when we feel very uncomfortable seeing our children struggle with their emotions and we want to stop the tantrum in some way or the other. But then, tantrums still become advantageous and children tend to repeat these more often to make you engage in those compensatory behaviours. Thus, it is important to be there for the child and not make the tantrum advantageous for them by compensating for it.

5. Undue attention to tantrums through dramatic reactions

Tantrums increase when we pay too much attention to them by making the situation very dramatic and interesting. This may look like the following:

a. All family members gather around the child during the tantrum and make it a big deal.

b. We overreact to the tantrum ourselves in terms of shouting at the child or getting too anxious.

When this happens, the behaviour of tantrums stays in the child's brain because of the associated reactions and they tend to repeat such behaviours. Also, when adults get very dysregulated around tantrums, it becomes really difficult for the child to regulate themselves.

6. Labelling our children as 'a child who throws tantrums'

This mostly happens when we get so worried about our children's tantrums that we start discussing their behaviour with others while our children are present and listening to us.

For example:

- Discussing the child's behaviour at school with the teacher when we go to pick up the child:
  'He has become so stubborn, he simply doesn't listen.'
- Discussing the child's behaviour with a relative on the phone:
  'She cries so much, I am so tired of it. I don't know what I should do.'
- Sometimes we even say things directly to children:
  'Why are you "always" acting stubborn?'
  'Why do you cry "so much"?'

When we label our children like this, they assume that 'this is the way I am' and they continue repeating that behaviour. So we must avoid discussing children's challenging behaviours around them if we do not want them to repeat those.

3

Tantrums Are Important

Tantrums seem to be very inconvenient in our daily routine with our kids, but do you know that they have an important role to play in our children's development?

Tantrums tell us what our children are feeling and what they need. There is always a reason underlying our children's tantrums!

Have you ever thought how, if there were no tantrums, would we ever know what our children are feeling? They cannot communicate in words about their emotions as they don't have the required language skills. Imagine a little child when they are born; they can only communicate through crying when hungry or uncomfortable. How else would we understand what they need if they didn't cry?

When a child throws a tantrum, they are expressing that they are not feeling good and need help. For example, I remember once when Saiveer came back from school. He was very cranky, unreasonable and defiant. I was finding it very difficult to keep my patience with him, but I could see something was up. After a couple of hours, he finally told me how he had cried in class that day because the teacher had scolded him. That's when I realized that he had had a hard day in school and that was the reason for his behaviour at home. I empathized with him and hugged him. Here, if I had lost my patience with my son, I wonder if he would have been able to open up about his school to me. I might have missed the reason underlying his behaviour.

Tantrums are necessary as they tell us when our children need our help and intervention. In fact, I would be more concerned about a child who does not throw tantrums at all, because that may mean that the child is not expressing his or her emotions and is instead suppressing them.

Children are always trying to communicate something to us through their behaviour.

In this section, I want to share with you a list of the most common reasons for children's tantrums increasing at home. I have put together this list after talking to numerous parents in my journey as a professional and also from my own experience. This list will help you understand your child's behaviour better and diagnose where the tantrums are coming from.

1. The child may be feeling overly corrected and thus frustrated.

This may come up in your behaviour towards your child in words such as this:

'Why are you shouting like that?'

'Don't run so fast.'

'Be careful, you need to do this slowly.'

'Stop speaking in that tone.'

'Stop jumping like this.'

No one likes to be corrected so much. Though I understand that the intention of the parent is to improve the child and their behaviour, when we overdo these corrections, the entire purpose is lost. Children stop feeling good about themselves and end up being crankier and throwing more tantrums.

When we over-correct our kids:

- they get irritated and stop responding to us;
- they start losing confidence because they feel they are not doing anything right;
- they feel powerless because they are being told what to do and what not to do all the time.

Correcting children is important, but the question is how much? I feel that any parent has the scope to cut down their corrections by at least half. I will discuss how to do that in the next section but till then, you can experiment with reducing your corrections and experience some positive changes!

2. The child may be feeling disconnected because the parent is losing patience very frequently and is irritable.

This is the most common reason that makes our children throw tantrums. When we parents lose our patience often and are mostly irritated in our tone with our children, they will throw more tantrums around us. If you observe your interactions with your child with an open mind, you will find this happening. Sometimes we as parents do not even realize that our behaviour with our child is changing. This generally happens when we are stressed out, unwell, burdened with a lot of work, or simply anxious about something.

For example, if you have been stressed since the morning and have been getting angry with your child because of that, you will end up seeing your child throwing more tantrums by the evening.

Observe this: *While putting your child to bed at night, when you end up getting irritated with them because they are taking too long to fall asleep, are they crankier when you wake them up next morning?*

So, whenever you feel your child is throwing a lot of tantrums, you need to check if you are throwing your own adult tantrums. I call it 'adult tantrums' because just like the child is unable to regulate their behaviour, so are we unable to modify ours. If adult tantrums increase, it in turn will lead to an increase in their children's tantrums.

Whenever I see my son's behaviour becoming weird in terms of acting out, becoming defiant or not listening and cooperating, my first thought is to check my own behaviour. I truly believe that my own anxiety and irritation affect my child's behaviour negatively. Sometimes my child helps me navigate my own behaviour and emotions!

3. The child may be feeling not understood due to a lack of empathy.

It is important for children to understand that whatever they are feeling is okay and valid. We ensure this by empathizing with them. But if we use sentences such as the following, we invalidate their emotions:

'Why are you crying like that, there is nothing to cry about.'

'Stop jumping like this, then I will talk to you.'

'You should understand and not get angry in this way.'

When we judge children for their feelings and keep explaining things to them instead of empathizing and connecting with their emotions, it leads to more tantrums.

Empathy means that we understand what the child is feeling, in spite of the situation. Our children are usually not even asking for logic or solutions, they just want to hear that 'we understand'. The situation may well be trivial for us, but we need to remember that the child's feelings are real and need to be validated. We cannot solve everything for our children, nor should we try to, but we can always connect with their emotions. (We will talk about 'how to empathize' in the next chapter in detail.)

4. The child may be struggling for attention and feels like tantrums are the way to get what they want.

Children require attention. It is their basic need. It makes them feel that they matter. A child struggling to get attention from family members will tend to throw more tantrums. First, because they are not feeling good due to the lack of attention and whatever they feel shows up in their behaviour as it is! And second, because their behaviour in the form of tantrums generally get them the attention they are seeking.

For example, a mother busy with work is unable to give time to the child, but the minute there is a tantrum, she leaves everything and attends to the child and gives her full attention. This tells the child that they need to cry or shout to get the mother's attention, and these behaviours start increasing.

When the negative behaviour of children receives more attention compared to their positive behaviour, negative behaviour will increase. Simply put, the behaviours that we pay attention to, increase.

Also, in case we give children what they want to stop the tantrum, they feel that tantrums are the way to get their demands fulfilled. It is not their fault that this is what they are learning. I will share my example here:

At bedtime, we have a rule that if we make it to bed on time, we read books together. But if we get late, we lose the time to read books. Once my son, Saiveer crossed his bedtime and started crying because he really wanted to read and couldn't. I realized that it was a holiday the next day and since it was not that late, I gave in to my son's demand and we read the book. Another time when we got late for bedtime, Saiveer started crying the same way as the previous day. I kept my calm and said, 'We still can't read the book, it is too late now.' At this point, he kept crying and said, 'But that day we read the book when I cried, why not today?' I had to control my laughter hearing him say this and said, 'But that is not how it is, baby.' Though he still tried his best to cry and change my decision, I had to be firm and let the tantrum pass so that he understood that crying was not going to help him here.

5. The child may be losing confidence due to unrealistic expectations and constant comparisons.

Sometimes, the reason a child throws tantrums is because what we are expecting them to do is something that they are not capable of doing and they end up getting irritated because of that. When our expectations become unrealistic, tantrums increase as the child feels incompetent, gets frustrated and gives up.

For example:

A mother complained that her three-year-old son was throwing a lot of tantrums when they practised his handwriting. When we talked further, we realized that her child was developmentally struggling to accomplish the task of writing as his fingers were not yet ready. Also, a child at the age of three is not able to sit in one place for too long to complete a task as they have a low attention span. These two reasons together were making the child rebel against writing. On the other hand, the mother was constantly comparing her son to other children who were able to write at the same age.

All children are different with unique temperaments and capabilities. When we constantly compare our children (with the thought of encouraging them to behave better), they stop feeling good about themselves and their behaviour gets worse instead of getting better. They feel they are not accepted for who they are.

In my experience with parents, this is very common in families with more than one child. If one of the children has a lot of energy or is strong-willed, they are often compared to the other child whose behaviour is comparatively easier to handle. The comparisons can easily sound like this:

'*Why don't you sit quietly like her?*'

'*This one does not listen to me at all.*'

'*This one is always stubborn, his sister is not like that.*'

When the child hears words like these, they start losing confidence in themselves. It may not be obvious from their behaviour because they will seem defiant and dysregulated, but internally they are suffering from low confidence as they feel that they are not liked. Another reason for a child's negative behaviours increasing is that these behaviours are highlighted so much in the family that it makes the child repeat them—again, we understand that this is because attention to a behaviour increases its instances.

6. The child may be hungry, overtired, overstimulated or overwhelmed by the sudden transition in their surroundings.

A child who is hungry or overtired will generally throw more tantrums. For example, if your child does not sleep well at night or is up way past their bedtime, they will behave in a dysregulated way. Also, if a child is overstimulated due to loud music or too many colours at a birthday party, they may throw more tantrums. By now, we have seen that this happens because children do not have a developed brain to regulate their emotions and when they are hungry, overtired or overstimulated, the efficiency of the behavioural filters in the brain decreases even more.

If we think about it, it happens to us too. When we are tired and exhausted, we start losing our patience with our children more easily because our own brain filters stop working effectively!

I would literally use this line with my son at times: 'Hungry mamma becomes angry mamma, so please let me eat, sweetheart.'

It is difficult for children to instantly adapt to new circumstances or routines as well. Therefore, the following situations may cause more tantrums in the child's behaviour:

- Shifting to a new house
- Having guests over
- A new sibling arriving in the family
- Going on a holiday
- A sudden change occurring in their routine
- Stress in the family (caused by death, divorce or crisis)

In such situations, we may feel that the child is acting in unreasonable ways, but actually, the child is unable to cope with the change and new surroundings and may also be overstimulated.

4

Aligning Our Expectations to How Our Children's Brains Work

After working with many parents, I have realized that some of the expectations that we have from our children are not aligned with their brain development. A child's brain is literally in the making—it is not completely formed. In fact, it is under construction for a long time after they are born.

A discussion on the anatomy of the brain is not within the scope of this book, nor am I an expert in the area of neuroscience. But, as a parent, I have realized that if we teach ourselves about two basic sets of information on children's brains, we will be able to make a lot of sense regarding what is going on with them.

Here I want to quote information from the book *The Whole Brain Child* by Daniel Siegel and Tina Payne Bryson:[1]

1. There is a left brain, the logical brain, which understands *language, words and logic*; and a right brain, the emotional brain, which understands *tone, emotions and gestures*. Our children's emotional brains are much more active than their logical brains (especially in their first three years).

2. The prefrontal cortex, called the 'upstairs brain', which is responsible for regulating emotions, is responsible for a lot of other aspects of behaviour like decision-making, empathy, focus and attention. This part develops fully only by the mid-twenties.

With this information, we can understand and solve the most common worries that parents have.

1. *My child does not focus and has a low attention span.*

It's normal!
Children's ability to focus keeps increasing as they grow and their brain develops. As we know, a six-year-old's attention span is much better than a three-year-old's as by then, the prefrontal cortex has developed more. Parents often get concerned when their three-year-old does not seem interested in the activities that they planned and gets distracted within ten minutes. This is very normal for a child at this age.

Children struggle to focus on any task for long durations and it is difficult for them to sit still for too long.

Also, different children develop at different rates, which means all three-year-olds will have varying individual attention spans.

I remember when Saiveer was three and a half, he had to attend online classes. He had a lot of energy and found it very difficult to sit in one place for too long and focus on class. I could see many children in his class sitting pretty easily and not struggling as much. When I started expecting the same from him, I saw him get even more dysregulated because he could not possibly sit still without moving. So, I had to modify my expectations of my son to be more realistic given his temperament. I allowed him breaks: to get up and move in the middle of the classes. I didn't get irritated when he could not sit for too long at a time. He had his own way of learning and I had to respect that. And when I adjusted my expectations according to his temperament, he started cooperating with me.

It is time we stop worrying about our children not paying attention and start building their focus patiently as they grow. (In case of concern, parents can always opt for a diagnosis of Attention Deficit/Hyperactivity Disorder. My point is that not all children having low attention spans necessarily have a disorder—mostly it is age-typical and should not be labelled as such, as that does more harm.)

2. *My two-year-old is unable to control his actions. I have told him so many times to not hit but he still does it.*

It's normal!
Children are very impulsive and will do things without thinking them through because of their developing prefrontal cortex. They will hit us even when they do not want to hurt us. They may regret it a minute later, but in that moment, they are unable to control the impulse. (We will talk about how to handle this in the discipline section.)

When Saiveer was five, we would do some worksheets together. I remember that sometimes, he would get so frustrated because of his own mistakes that he would end up scribbling on the whole sheet and a moment later say, 'I didn't want to do that, please clean it.'

Our little children are unable to see through the consequences of their behaviour. If you see a four-year-old trying to put a lot of water in a small bottle and making a total mess, know that this is completely normal. If your seven-year-old wants to wear a jacket to school on a hot summer day, it is because their brain cannot process all the information and make a logical decision. So, do not judge them for their poor decision-making; it will improve as they grow up.

3. *My child is unable to tell me what he is feeling or what he did in school.*

It's normal!
Due to our children's developing brains, it is difficult for them to organize their thoughts and put them into

words to express what they are thinking. This is the reason children are unable to tell parents about their day at school when parents ask, 'How was your day? What did you do?'

Instead, it is helpful to ask specific questions like 'Who sat with you today?' or 'Did you go to the playground today?' They may take more time to frame their sentences; being patient and pausing instead of prompting repeatedly (for example, 'Tell me, why are you not telling me') gives children space to express themselves. Sometimes they may answer after a few minutes as well if we do not pester.

As children grow and their brains develop, they will be able to express themselves better through language. And when we give them the necessary emotional connection, it helps them to open up and share more and more.

4. *My child does not consider others' feelings and seems very self-centred.*

It's normal!
It is difficult for children to understand what other people are feeling because they are not experiencing that emotion themselves. As they grow and their brain develops further, they learn that their thoughts and emotions may be different from others. This is the reason when we ask children questions like 'Do you know that child is feeling bad because you are not sharing your toys?', it does not make sense to them, and sharing does not come naturally.

Basically, children are unable to see things from other people's perspective in the early years. For example, my five-year-old hides behind the table where I can see most of his body but he thinks he is not visible to me. He cannot see the situation from my perspective.

Considering others' feelings and seeing things from other people's perspectives is a skill that children are just learning. We can help them learn this skill by showing respect to their emotions and empathizing with them, and also by modelling understanding other people's feelings and sharing with them ('I think papa is very tired and that is why he got irritated, maybe he needs some rest and will feel better afterwards').

Remember, all children are different and may learn this skill at different ages. You may see children as young as three showing empathy, and some children learn this skill when they are six or seven years old.

Learning more about our children's brains does help us in many ways to broaden our perspective, have more realistic expectations from them and be more patient with them.

II
CONNECTION

5

Why Don't Our Children Listen to Us?

'My child does not listen to me.'
'My child ignores me completely.'
'I have to repeat everything ten times before my child pays attention.'
'I have to get angry to get her to do every small task, or else she doesn't care.'
'I explain things so much, but my child still does not understand.'

As parents, we are responsible for our children and need their cooperation to fulfil that responsibility. There are so many things we need to get done—from waking up our children in the morning, making them eat and study, managing their behaviour and keeping them safe, to putting them to sleep at the end of the day! How can we accomplish all this without them cooperating with us?

Parenting turns out to be the most difficult when we struggle to get our children to do even everyday tasks. It gets frustrating when we instruct them to do something or correct their actions and they do not respond and follow. We often feel so helpless that we lose our temper with them, and even end up arguing. Our homes look more like a battlefield where we have to struggle and fight for everything.

Though we understand that our children's brains are still developing, we do need these little brains to cooperate with us; how else will we function as parents? After all, we do everything for our children and have the best intentions for them. Why, then, are children unable to see that? Why don't they listen to us? What can be the reason behind them being defiant?

Children stop listening to us when they feel disconnected from us.
If we want our children to cooperate with us, we need to build more of a connection with them.

Yes, it is that simple! I know you might not be very convinced about this right now and may even be thinking, 'I am already connected to my child.' But please keep reading; you will soon see what I mean and get your answers.

First of all, I want to emphasize that here, what I mean by connection is different from love. I believe every parent loves their child deeply. Love already exists in the relationship; that is why you are reading this book in the first place—out of your loving concern for your child. But there can still be a lack of connection despite the love in the relationship.

Let us see how we can identify the **disconnection** in our relationships with our children, which in turn will help us better understand what connection is:

There is a disconnection if you are facing one or more of these issues:

- Your child consistently does not listen to you.
- You are unable to get through to your child.
- Your child has become immune to your anger.
- You have to take the help of other people to get things done by your child.
- Your child does not want to spend time with you.
- Your child complains, 'You don't love me' or 'You don't understand me'.

How does 'connection' play an important role here? Connection helps us in three ways:

1. It gets our message across to our children.
2. It gives us more influence over our children's decisions.
3. It saves us from being the bad guy, in spite of being the rule-maker.

Let's elaborate on these points to understand:

1. Connection gets our message across to our children.

If we understand the simple meaning of the word 'connection', it is a link between two things to get something across. For example, when two wires are connected, it is possible to get electricity from one to the other. Or, when we have a phone connection, our text or voice messages can get to the other end. The flow stops the minute there is a disconnection.

Likewise, for our children to receive our messages, instructions, love, explanations and logic, we need a connection in the relationship. We may have the best intentions for our children, but the child may not be able to see or receive it because of the 'disconnect'.

Let's say that while I am taking an online workshop, I lose my internet connection and don't even realize it at that moment. I continue speaking and feel disheartened that no one is responding before I realize that there is a disconnection and my messages have stopped reaching my audience. Here, does it make sense for me to continue speaking, or will it make more sense to sort out the internet connection first?

Similarly, let's imagine that you are instructing your six-year-old from a distance saying, 'Stop playing and wear your shoes', and your child is not responding. You can either continue to shout from a distance ten times or you can just go up to the child, kneel to their level, put a hand on their shoulder and say, 'I love these cars you are playing with; looks so interesting; but we need to wear our shoes now. Do you need my help?' This may just increase the odds that your child will respond to you more positively. What do you think changed here? Well, our message in the instructions got across because of the connection we just made. How will the child cooperate if they are not even receiving our messages due to a disconnection?

2. It gives us more influence over our children's decisions.

This is the most appealing advantage for most parents. A connection gives us more influence over our children's behaviour, which means that when we have a connection,

- children cooperate with us more and we don't have to get angry with them about everything;
- they say 'yes' to us more often;
- they listen to us more and even follow more rules with lesser resistance.

Don't we all want this influence? Won't our life get easier if our children were a little more willing to cooperate with us? What happens when we lose this influence?

Here, I want to pose an important question to my readers: **Can we control our children's behaviour?**

Many assume that we can control our children's behaviour to a certain extent. After all, we are the parents, and our children are too young to make decisions on their own. So we must control their actions to keep them safe and to teach them the correct values.

Consider this example:

You have to make your five-year-old complete a worksheet in which she has to write the letter 'A' five times. You sharpen the pencil and place the worksheet in front of your child; you tell her to hold the pencil correctly and write to complete the task. In case your child does not cooperate, you may try the following ways to make your child do the work:

- *You can try to explain to your child why it is essential for them to complete the worksheet.*
- *You can offer a bribe: 'I will give you a chocolate if you write.'*
- *You can try to get angry and raise your voice to scare them into doing the work.*
- *You can try to threaten them by withholding something they like: 'If you don't write, I will not take you out.'*
- *You may even try corporal punishment, such as hitting the child, to force them to write. (Please note, I do not recommend this under any circumstances, and it is even illegal in some countries.)*

You can try to implement all these techniques to ensure that your child does the work, but who decides whether your child actually picks up the pencil and writes the letter 'A' on the worksheet? Who ultimately decides to move the hand, hold the pencil and start writing? In spite of all your efforts, if your child chooses not to understand that explanation, does not take that bribe, does not respond to your anger, threat or even physical punishment, and decides not to move their hands, then what can you do?

So, let's think again: Can we really control our children's behaviour?

In reality, the answer is that we can't. Sometimes, we mistakenly think we can control their behaviour because our children are allowing us to do so, reacting to our show of anger and force. But the day they decide, 'I am not going to cooperate in spite of the anger or even the hitting', we will realize that we can't really make them do anything they don't want to. For example, we cannot make them say the word 'sorry' if they decide not to say it, no matter how hard we try.

Thus, we do need more influence over our children to help them cooperate with us as we can't really control their behaviour, at least not in the long term.

When we work on building a connection in any relationship, our influence increases over the other person. The power of connection holds true in any relationship.

Let's examine the connection in a husband–wife relationship:

Imagine that in a household, there is a husband and a wife. The husband has to travel to the office to work and the wife works from home. Thus, it so happens that the wife mostly takes care of the house during the day. One morning, the couple has an argument where the husband complains that in spite of being home, the wife is not managing the house well. He points out his wife's mistakes, at which the wife feels offended and complains that she is working long hours herself. After the distasteful argument, they continue with the day as planned. That very evening, the husband needs his wife's support in entertaining a few of his clients over dinner at home. So, he calls her to inform her and requests her to prepare dinner plans. Do you think the wife will want to cooperate here? She may even refuse to help and spitefully say to her spouse, 'I am not helping you here; please manage on your own.'

Now imagine another situation where the husband, before leaving for the office in the morning, decides to take out time to appreciate his spouse for managing everything beautifully in spite of juggling a busy work schedule. The wife naturally gets a confidence boost and the couple feels good about their relationship, bringing more positivity into it. Later in the evening, if the husband calls and asks the wife for support for entertaining clients for dinner, do you think the wife's response will change this time? Maybe she will cooperate with a smile and want to do it for him because her husband just got more influence over her behaviour.

The circumstances may change and gender roles can be reversed depending on the situation, but the point here is that when one spouse builds more connection with the other, they have a greater chance of influencing their partner.

As parents, there are times when we use such sentences:

'My child listens to her grandmother more.'

'My child does not eat when I feed him but will eat when the nanny feeds him.'

'I have to request the teacher to convince my child.'

Here, we see that the child cooperates more with another person than the parent. If a person other than a parent is able to make the child do something and influence their actions, then it indicates that this person has more connection in their relationship with the child. The key takeaway is that it is also possible for us parents to build a similarly strong connection with our children and increase our influence over them.

3. Connection saves us from being the bad guy, in spite of being the rule-maker.

We are the parents, and we automatically become the ones to enforce all the rules and boundaries over our children. We are regulating their screen time, their eating habits, their studies, their behaviour and so on. When we consciously invest in building connections with our children, we can have a beautiful relationship with them in spite of doing all the above and our children tend to rebel less often. This happens because, with increased connection in the relationship, our true intentions and genuine love get across as well.

When there is a strong connection in a parent–child relationship, it looks like this:

- The child feels good about the relationship that he/she shares with the parents.
- The child feels good about themselves around their parents.
- The child feels accepted, heard, validated and respected.
- There is much more positivity in the relationship.

Building a connection does not necessarily mean giving in to our children's every demand and pampering them. We can have a strong connection despite the rules and boundaries we set for our kids. (You will understand how this works once you have read the entire section on connection and positive discipline.)

Now, the main question arises: How do we build this connection?

We are already doing so much for our children and love them deeply. What else can we do? Where are we lacking? Is there something we are missing? This is what I am going to answer in detail in the next chapter. I will help you to see the root causes of the issues in our daily interactions that may go unnoticed, just because we don't even know that they matter; but these same are very simple to correct. I will suggest easy-to-understand yet extremely effective ways to build this connection with our children using real-life examples that will give you hands-on practical tools to help your children listen to you and cooperate more. **Remember, we cannot control our children's behaviour but we can influence their behaviour with the help of connection.**

6

How Can We Build a Connection with Our Children?

The nature of any relationship that we see around us is manifested through the forms of communication that the people in that relationship engage in, that is, how they talk to and behave with each other. There are so many parent–child relationships we see, but are they all the same? No. They differ in the kind of interactions that the parent and the child engage in with each other. For example, some relationships may have more arguments involving irritable words and tones, while others may have more empathy and a respectful communication pattern.

We are interacting with our children in some way or the other during the whole time we are around them. Let us categorize these interactions as either positive (those that prompt a healthy response from the parent and the child) or negative (those that produce stress in the parent and the child). This is what these positive and negative interactions look like in the day-to-day interactions with our children:

Negative interactions	Positive interactions
Scolding	Listening to the child
Correcting	Playing
Taunting	Laughing
Comparing	Praising
Explaining (lecturing)	Empathizing and validating

- Now take a minute, close your eyes, imagine any ordinary day with your child and reflect: 'How many positive interactions and how many negative interactions do I have with my child in a day?'
- 'What is the ratio of positive to negative interactions I have with my child?' (You may be spending more time or less time with your child, but during the time you spend with them, what is the ratio of positive to negative interactions?)
- 'How many times do I correct my child, and how many times do I praise my child? How many times do I scold my child and how many times do I laugh with my child?'

According to relationship researcher John Gottman, to have an affirming and connected relationship with a partner, we need to have the magic ratio of 1:5

negative to positive interactions.[2] This means that for every negative interaction, we need to have five positive interactions. This ratio is true for any bond and works most beautifully in the parent–child relationship. When we consciously work on increasing the ratio of positive interactions compared to negative interactions, we can effectively increase the connection in the relationship with our children.

What this also means is that no matter how much time you are spending with your child, it is this ratio of positive to negative interactions that truly determines what kind of connection you have. You may be a working parent who is not able to spend more than two hours on a weekday with your child or you could be a stay-at-home parent who spends most of your day around your child; in each case, it is the quality of the time spent that matters in terms of building a connection.

Remember: For every negative interaction, we need to have five positive interactions with our children!

Now, I understand that it is not easy to achieve such a golden ratio. Most of us parents don't even get close to this ratio because we are so busy raising children and parenting them that we forget to focus on the relationship part. We are so occupied with giving them the right values and taking care of their health and education that we miss out on connecting with them.

I remember that when I read about this ratio, my son was only one and a half years old and the ratio of my interactions with him was way off at the time. When I started to consciously work on the quality of my interactions with my son, I began to see how achievable the golden ratio of 1:5 is and how it really brings magic to the relationship. Not only does it bring about more cooperation from our children, but it also gifts us the beautiful relationship with our children we all wish for.

Now that we have understood why a connection with our children is absolutely necessary and also learnt about the interaction ratio, I will share with you some practical ways to reach this golden ratio and build a strong connection. After all, the main question is: 'How can we be so positive with our children when they don't listen to us in the first place?'

Here are seven ideas you can start following to see your relationship with your child transform. Even if you choose to work with only three of the ideas out of the seven that we will discuss and start experimenting with, you will see a massive change in your relationship with your child and in your child's cooperation.

1. Show more respect

Again, do not confuse respect with love. We may love our children with all our hearts, but still not show them enough respect. If we reflect on the following questions with an open mind, we will get more clarity about how much respect we truly show to our little ones.

- *How do I talk to my child, and how do I talk to other people? Is there a difference in the tone or choice of words?*
- *Am I more patient with other people (especially when they do something I don't like) and not as much with my own child?*
- *How irritated and impatient do I get with my child, especially if I am exhausted or stressed out? Do I do this with other people?*

Our children are constantly watching us behave this way—even if they do not say anything, they are observing, comprehending and forming their own opinions. So, we need to be more mindful of all our interactions.

Another point we need to observe is how we talk about and discuss our children with other people. That is another way to assess if we are being respectful towards our children. Do we say such things as:

- *'She is so shy; she just doesn't want to speak in front of anyone. Other children in the class are so active and involved.'*
- *'He is so stubborn; he doesn't want to understand anything. His sister is nothing like him. She is very well-behaved.'*

The most common reason why we talk about our children in this way is because we worry about their behaviour and often want to share our concerns with others in the hope of receiving advice. But if we say such things within earshot of our children, you have to agree that that is not a very respectful thing to do. Overhearing negative words like these makes children lose confidence in themselves. We often assume that our children are not paying attention to our conversations, but trust me, they are always listening if they are around, no matter what age. They may be playing in one corner of the room while you are talking about them, but they are definitely listening.

Respect is an essential part of every relationship. When we consciously start giving respect to our children in the way we talk to them and talk about them, it helps us build a beautiful connection with them. We should also cultivate the habit of being consciously respectful to our children because of the following reasons:

a. When we give respect to our children, it shows them that they deserve respect

Children need to feel respected in their own homes and to know that they are worthy of receiving respect. This is very important for their development because they will learn to allow people to treat them in the same way that they are treated at home. **It is at home that the foundation for their self-esteem is laid.**

I want to share the real-life experience of a client here.

A parent was concerned that her six-year-old was not taking a stand among his friends whenever

negative interactions occurred. Once she happened to see that her son's friends were blaming him for doing something that he had not done. The mother was very surprised to find that her son kept quiet and didn't defend himself at all. When she asked her child later, 'Why did you not say anything in your defence?' he went completely quiet.

The mother then informed me that her husband had left her two years before and she had been going through a very tough time. She was in a new country and living alone with her child. She accepted the fact that she had not been very nice to her son during this challenging time. She had been disrespectful and demeaning and was often impatient and irritated with the child.

It was clear to me that this had made the boy lose all confidence in himself. He didn't see any point in speaking up for himself because he could see that his mother never supported him or spoke in his favour. The child had learnt to believe that it was normal to be treated in this way, even by others. When the mother realized the impact of her behaviour towards her son, she significantly changed her interactions with him to help him regain his self-esteem.

b. When children receive respect, they learn to give respect to others

It is tough for a child to learn respectful words and behaviour if they don't see people modelling it around them. The most common evidence of this can be found when we observe siblings interacting with one another. A parent who gets angry or loses patience a lot will see their elder child behaving in similar ways towards the younger sibling. But if the same parent is respectful with their elder one, the elder child will learn to treat the younger one that way too. Children always learn what they see and receive.

c. When we are respectful towards our children, other people treat our children respectfully as well

When we treat our children with respect in front of others, other people talk to our children in similar ways. If you always find and point out your child's faults, so will others around you. If you get angry at your child a lot, you will see other people using the same tone to deal with your child. On the other hand, if you give respect to your child, you will see people changing the way they talk to your child too. In a way, we are laying down the standards of communication for our child. There is no incentive for a third person to behave well with a child if the child's parents are not respectful towards them. Others modify behaviour towards our child based on what they think you will accept and tolerate.

2. Regulate your behaviour

How often do we lose our patience with our children, and how diligently do we try to regulate our behaviour with them?

How many times do we regret shouting at our child just because we were stressed out and couldn't control ourselves?

I empathize entirely with the parents in this case. I understand that we cannot be perfectly calm all the time; after all, we are human beings and deal with so many pressures in our lives every day. There will obviously be times when we won't be able to regulate ourselves. But the big questions are: 'How many times and to what extent are we getting dysregulated and losing control over our words and actions when we are interacting with our children? What is our pattern of communication with them? Even if we apologize for our behaviour, are we repeating it and unknowingly ending up in a vicious cycle?

Our behaviour exerts a lot of influence over our children's behaviour. When we don't regulate our own behaviour, express our irritation in our tone and actions often, react to the slightest provocation and are impatient in our dealings with our children, we see an increase in the instances of tantrums and defiance in them as well.

Children end up feeling and behaving in this way because they do not feel good about themselves when we adults behave impatiently with them. As children are not capable of filtering their emotions and whatever they feel is reflected in their actions as it is, it is no wonder that they throw tantrums or display challenging behaviour when they do not feel good. Moreover, when we adults are dysregulated and not in control of our emotions, children too get dysregulated merely by observing and being around us, and even copying our behaviour. So, it is very important that we work on managing our emotions to build a connection with our children and help them listen to us.

If we think about it, we do manage our behaviour with other people most of the time—at our workplace, with our friends and family, and even with strangers. In spite of being stressed out, we will often effectively manage to regulate while we are talking to other adults. But our tone and behaviour change when we interact with our children and we may become impatient and irritated more easily. Somehow, we think that it's okay to be like that with our kids. But in truth, it only worsens our situation. (We will talk about how we can regulate ourselves and learn to be calmer in greater detail in the 'calm' section of the book.)

3. Listen, validate and empathize

When we listen to our children without being distracted, validate what they are feeling instead of judging their emotions and genuinely empathize with them, we can form a deep emotional connection with them. This is a simple way to communicate with our kids and if we adopt this technique, it will help us form a beautiful bond with them.

Let us elaborate on what these behaviours should look like in our daily interactions and in moments of challenge with our children:

a. **Listen:** It is such a simple parenting tip to say,
    'Listen to your children'. But at times, we are so
    busy in our lives and our day-to-day commitments
    that we miss out on following this. If we carefully
    observe our interactions with our kids, we will
    realize that we, more often than not, end up
    instructing them, explaining things to them and
    urging them to complete the tasks at hand—but it
    is not as regularly that we listen to them.

    Have you noticed how, when children are talking,
    we start explaining things to them or giving them
    a lecture? This causes the child to lose interest in
    sharing with us what they originally intended. For
    example, suppose the child says, 'Today I copied my
    friend's work in the class.' Here, instead of exploring
    what they mean by asking more questions such
    as 'Really, which work?', 'How did you copy?' or
    saying things like, 'It was nice of your friend to help
    you', we may immediately start lecturing them by
    saying, 'We should not copy others' work' and 'You
    should do your own work'. When we start lecturing
    our children too much, they may start tuning us
    out, paying absolutely no attention to what we are
    saying. Worse still, as they grow, they may start
    hiding things from us to avoid being lectured.

    Practise having conversations with your children
    where you consciously show curiosity and interest
    when they share something with you and ask
    them exploratory questions to help them express
    themselves. Your prompts should sound something
    like these:

'Oh really, that happened?'
'What did your friend say then?'
'That sounds so funny' (and then maybe even laugh together).

In my sessions with parents, I have helped them change themselves from being lecture-giving parents to parents who listen effectively, and that has helped their relationships with their children tremendously. Thus, to be more connected with your child, pay more attention to them when they speak. If you do have a moment to spare, physically get down to their level (like sitting or kneeling next to them), look into their eyes and say the words, 'Yes, sweetheart, tell me, what do you want to say?' and then listen. Pause and be patient as your child puts their thoughts into words—it takes them time to do so. Allow them at least thirty seconds and say nothing, wait for your child to speak and you will see your child sharing more and more with you.

b. **Validate the feelings**: While listening, we need to validate the feelings that children express and not judge them for what they feel. This is especially true when they are upset about something. In such situations avoid these words:
'There is nothing to be upset about.'
'Why are you getting angry?'
'You should not feel jealous like this.'
'Don't feel so bad about losing, it's okay.'
Firstly, we need to remind ourselves that none of us can control what we feel; feelings just happen. When

we say things like the above, we end up judging our children for their emotions. Children then get confused and end up suppressing their feelings instead of dealing with them in a healthy way. They also do not feel understood and connected to us when we judge them like this or dismiss how they might feel. It is very important to tell children that it is okay to feel angry, jealous, disappointed or upset—we can try by using words such as the following:

'*I can see you got angry.*'

'*We all get upset sometimes.*'

'*I think you felt jealous; it happens.*'

'*I think you are feeling upset because you lost. It happens to all of us. I can understand.*'

Remember, experiencing emotions is part of being a human being—it is what we do with these emotions that is important. For example, it is natural to be angry, even as parents, but how we behave during the time we are angry is important. This is what we can help our children learn when we validate their emotions.

c. **Empathize:** When children share a problem with us, we as parents generally feel obligated to give them a solution or provide some explanation for it. But we have to realize that we cannot solve everything for our children. Also, children are already tired of listening to lectures and explanations from everyone; they do not want more of that.

They typically need someone to understand what they are going through. Let's take an example:

Suppose your child comes to you very upset saying, 'My toy just broke.' We can respond in the following ways in this situation:

Response without empathy	Response with empathy
Parent: 'It's okay, we will buy a new one.' Child: 'No, I want one now!' Parent: 'You should be careful while playing. I cannot go to the market now.' Child: 'Fix this.' Parent: 'I cannot fix it.' The child is crying now. Parent: 'First, stop crying; crying won't fix the car. There are so many more cars; you can play with those.' The child is still crying, 'I only want to play with this car.' Parent: 'Be more careful next time. I can't do anything. We will buy another one later.' And so on . . .	Parent: 'Really? Show me.' Once you see it. 'Yes, it does look broken, oh!' Child: 'Fix it right now.' Parent: 'I wish I could, but It doesn't seem it can be fixed.' Child: 'I want it to be fixed. Why did it break?' Parent: 'Oh, you seem upset; you really liked this car.' Child: 'Yes, I did.' And starts crying. The parent lets the child express it. Parent: 'I know baby, this is hard.' The parent hugs the child (if the child wants to be hugged). In case the child says, 'I want a new one.' The parent can respond, 'I know you do, but we can't buy a new toy right now. Come here, I think you need a hug.'

Let's take another situation. Your child comes to you complaining, 'My teacher scolded me at school today.'

Response without empathy	Response with empathy
Parent: 'Why, what did you do?' Child: 'I was not paying attention and she scolded me.' Parent: 'You should pay attention in class.' Child: 'I cried in the class.' Parent: 'Why did you cry? Pay attention next time so ma'am will not scold you.' The child might not know how to respond here and may even stop sharing at this point.	Parent: 'Really, what happened?' Child: 'I was not paying attention and she scolded me.' Parent: 'Oh, did you feel bad when she scolded you?' Child: 'Yes, I cried.' Parent: 'You had a hard day it seems. It happens at school sometimes, I am here for you, come.' Child: 'Then ma'am called me to her and hugged me.' Parent: 'That's nice of her. Let me also give you a hug.'

When we approach the situation with empathy, children can express what they feel more effectively and give us more information as well.

Here, I want to reinforce two points that we have already discussed in an earlier part of the book:

- We do not have to over-empathize, that is, we do not need to keep repeating our words of empathy again and again.

- We have to make sure that our empathy is genuine,
  and that it is present in our body, expressions and
  tone. Children can sense it when we don't mean
  what we say.*

To conclude this point, I want to emphasize that
empathy should be used more often in our day-to-day
conversations with our children. When we empathize,
we connect with our child's emotional brain, which helps
them access their logical brain. This makes children feel
better and allows them to make better decisions too.

4. **How we respond to our children's mistakes
   determines how connected our children feel**

Children are going to make many mistakes. For that
matter, we all make mistakes. But, since our children
have developing brains and are under adult supervision
all the time, their mistakes look different to us and are
highlighted a lot more.

For example, if an adult spills water, we don't
react much, but when a child spills water, we may get
impatient and say, 'That is why I tell you to be careful!
See, it is all wet now.' We forget that if an adult who
has fully developed motor skills can still spill water
sometimes, it is only natural that children are more

---

* These points have been discussed in the first section of the
  book and have already been elaborated in detail as 'using
  empathy during tantrums' in that section.

likely to have such accidents because their hands and coordination skills are still developing.

When children make a mistake and are confronted with it, it is a very unpleasant moment for them. This is because they are emotionally vulnerable at such times. Picture your child's expression during such a moment: they are literally asking you, maybe without using the words, 'Is it bad? Can I trust you not to insult me? I am scared.'

Most kids know they have messed up, even when they still behave irrationally after making a mistake. Their irrational behaviour can be attributed to the fact that they don't know how to handle their fear of being reprimanded and are trying to understand if they are safe.

Therefore, it is essential that we do not disrespect them for their mistakes or label them a 'bad' child. Instead, we must empathize with them and tell them that although they have messed up, it doesn't make them a bad person. We have to be respectful even while setting a boundary or deciding the consequences of a child's actions. We must always believe in the child's inner goodness.

When we do that, our children believe that they can lean on us for support if they ever get into trouble in life. They are reassured that we are capable of handling the situation and will keep loving them no matter what.

But if we fail to instil this confidence in our children by being disrespectful towards them, we create a disconnect with them. We risk losing their trust and with time, they are likely to resort to lying to protect themselves from our negative reactions. This is a very common issue faced by parents who are, very often, hard on their children for their mistakes.

We cannot have children who never make mistakes, nor do we want them to be too scared of making mistakes, for then they will start losing confidence. Remember, children will make a lot of mistakes in their lives—it helps them to learn from the consequences of them. During our parenting journey, we will have to face situations where our children may use a bad word, do something untoward in school or react in some way that is not appropriate. Yes, we will need to help them understand and guide them in such situations, but we do not have to judge them and make them feel bad about it. To make things simpler, ask yourself, how would *you* want someone to talk to you after you make a mistake? You'd want them to be patient and forgiving with you and trust that you will learn from your experience. It must be the same for your reaction to your children.

5. Choose your fights and correct children less often

As parents, we feel so responsible for our kids that we always keep correcting their behaviour. It comes across in words like this:

 'Don't run so fast.'
 'Eat carefully; your clothes are getting dirty.'
 'Be careful, you may get hurt.'
 'Don't put your finger in your mouth.'
 'Don't talk in that tone.'
 'Why are you touching that box, it is empty.'

'Play with your toy properly, it will break.'
'Don't move your hands like this.'

We aim to improve our children but correcting them too much and too often does not help us move towards that goal. Instead, it disconnects us from our children due to the following reasons:

- When we correct our children too often, they get frustrated. After all, they cannot behave according to our wishes and standards all the time. So, over-correction leads to more tantrums as kids begin to feel inferior and may even stop paying any heed to us.
- If we get in the habit of correcting them too much, children start muting us when we say something. They stop responding to what we are saying and our words begin to lose value. In such situations, our most likely reaction is to resort to shouting, which further disconnects us from them.
- We soon notice that the behaviour we correct too frequently actually starts recurring more often. This is because correction is also a form of attention being paid to the behaviour.
- Children lose confidence in themselves when corrected too often as they feel they are not doing anything right. They stop feeling good about themselves, especially around us, leading to a disconnect in the relationship.

Hence, it is important that we consciously choose our fights, thus reducing our negative interactions with

our children and correcting them less. We can choose
which behaviours to correct on the following basis:

- Overlook behaviours that are not harmful
  Avoid correcting behaviours that do not harm
  anyone. When choosing which behaviours are
  important to instil properly, we can ignore
  behaviours that are not harmful. For example, we
  must correct our child if they hit others or break
  something or when they do not do their homework,
  but we can avoid correcting them when they are
  just being loud, jumping here and there, or even
  changing their clothes four times a day. After all,
  children are going to behave like children.

- Understand your child and be realistic
  It is important for each parent to understand their
  child's unique temperament as well as capabilities
  and have realistic expectations from them. For
  example, I know my six-year-old has a lot of energy
  and it is difficult for him to sit still. But if I keep
  telling him to sit properly over and over when we
  are at a restaurant, he will end up feeling irritated.
  So, I choose to ignore situations where he keeps
  fidgeting or getting up from the chair repeatedly.

When we consciously choose the instances to correct
our children, understand and accept them and have
realistic expectations from them while being patient,
we become successful in building a strong connection
in our relationship with them.

6. Be more optimistic about children and praise them often

Children are always looking for approval from their parents and caregivers. When they receive our approval and positive attention, they feel good about themselves. This gives their confidence a boost and leads them to believe that they are worthy human beings. This also helps in building our connection with them as they feel good about themselves around us. Remember, our children are always paying attention to things they hear us say (even when we don't realize it) and our words have an immense impact on their overall personality. Children become what we tell them they are; thus, our words hold a lot of value. Therefore, we need to be more encouraging and optimistic while describing our children's behaviour.

So, choose your words wisely. Here are a few examples:

Instead of saying:	Say:
'My child is shy.'	*'My child takes some time before she opens up.'*
'My child is very hyper.'	*'My child has a lot of energy and when that is channelized, he does wonders.'*
'She is so stubborn.'	*'She has a strong will and feels emotions deeply.'*
'She cries a lot.'	*'She is learning to deal with her emotions.'*

It is important to praise our children for their efforts as they need to feel appreciated to build their confidence and self-esteem.

Let's think for a minute: *How much are we correcting our children, and in comparison, how often are we praising them?*

All children have their own strengths and weaknesses. When we praise a child, we highlight their strengths and when we correct them, we highlight their weaknesses. What should we highlight more? Surely, the strengths!

Here are a few points I want to reinforce regarding praising children:

- **Praise should be genuine:** False praise is never effective. Tell them what they actually do well instead of just saying something to make them feel good or to make them cooperate.

   For example, when your child does not want to go to his classes and you want to encourage him to go, you might say in false praise: *'My son plays badminton so well. He loves going to his classes.'*

   Instead, try offering this genuine praise: *'My son is learning to play badminton. His interest will grow with time. I am so proud of him that he is going every day.'*

- **Do not over-praise:** We need to praise children enough and not too much. Over-praising either makes children overconfident or addicted to praise (when they need praise to feel good all the time).

So, do not routinely start praising children but genuinely appreciate them wherever you can.

- **Make praise more descriptive:** When you are praising your child, go beyond the words, 'You are such a good boy/girl'. Be more descriptive about the behaviour that you are praising. Say something like, 'The way you have coloured the blue whale is so creative'.

- **Observe how your child likes to be praised:** Some children may not enjoy effusive praises. They might feel conscious and stop doing what they are doing when praised. So, we must be more subtle with these kids. Observe and understand how your child likes to be praised and tailor your words according to that.

7. Play with your child

Playing with children is a highly effective way of engaging with them and building a stronger connection. When we consciously take out thirty minutes of one-on-one playtime with our children every day, they feel good and secure about their relationship with us. Playing with our children also helps us to accumulate many positive interactions in a short span of time.

I encourage you to include this time in your daily routine—it can be in the evening or at bedtime, or if you are a working parent, it can be a special time during the weekends.

Make sure you follow these points to make playtime effective:

- **No distractions:** Keep your gadgets and work aside, and pay full attention to the child.
- **No ulterior motives:** The agenda at playtime should purely be to build that *connection*. Even if you plan an activity and your child doesn't want to do it, then you must **follow your child's lead** and play whatever games they want to play. That may turn out to be something that doesn't even make sense to you, but if it is fun for them, go along with it.

  I remember how my son would ask me to sit on his plastic scooter and go to each room and pretend to buy something from there. And when I did that with him, he felt very good and connected to me.

- **Make this time fun:** To make playtime fun, we need to be patient. There should be fewer corrections and instructions at this time. For example, when I paint with my child, I make sure he is wearing clothes that he can get dirty so that I do not have to tell him to be careful about spilling colour on them. Another time when I planned an activity using glue and craft paper, my son wanted to explore the sensation of the stickiness of glue. We could not even complete the planned activity because the glue itself fascinated my son so much. I let him enjoy that moment and the new sensations instead of pushing him to participate in the activity that I had planned. It is essential that children feel loved and accepted during play and that should be the main agenda of that time.

Children need to know that you are having fun too: Let them know how much you love spending time with them. Let your child feel special through your words. Avoid saying something like, 'If you do this, then I will not play with you'. The purpose of playtime is lost when we use such words as they feel we are not really enjoying the time together with them but doing this out of duty or compulsion. In case you find it necessary to enforce a boundary, here's an example of how that can be done. Say, your child is putting paint on the wall and you cannot allow it, you can say, 'We cannot dirty the walls like this. If we do this then, we will not be able to continue painting together, and I don't want to miss this fun time with you.'

When we take some time out to connect through play with our children, we start to see its effect in other interactions with our children as well. We see their cooperation increase and how they are in a better mood throughout the day. This happens because they feel validated through our positive interactions and the attention they receive during playtime, which leads to them feeling good about themselves and their connection with us.

Remember, children also want to share a beautiful relationship with us parents just like we do with them. Sometimes, we start believing that our children do not want to cooperate and are deliberately making it challenging for us. But this is not the case. In reality, they need help from us in the form of connection. Children need more acceptance and patience from our end—when we give them that, we see a beautiful side of them.

7

The Added Benefits of Building Connections with Our Children

Building connections with our children not only gets us cooperation from them but has many more advantages.

1. A connection helps us to balance out our negative interactions

It is bound to happen that at one time or the other, we will lose our patience with our children or have a negative episode with them. In such situations, instead of feeling guilty, we should look at connection theory for direction—we just need to have more positive interactions to balance that negative interaction.

This does not mean we must compensate for our behaviour by giving gifts, giving into a child's unreasonable demands or going out of our way to show we are sorry. Instead, we need to find simple opportunities to connect in earnest with our children.

For example, when I have a negative interaction with my child, I balance it by having more positive interactions in the following ways:

- I go up to my child and say something like:
  - *'This is the T-shirt we bought last week, right? It looks good on you!'*
  - *'Are you making a flower? I like the yellow petals; it looks like a sunflower.'*
- I express my fondness towards him:
  - *'You are my favourite person; can I get a hug?'*
  - *'I hope you know that you are very special to me.'*
- If I have the time, I play with my child for a while and accumulate many more positive interactions with him.

When we consistently work on our connection with our children in our day-to-day lives, the base of our relationship becomes stronger. When we have a strong foundation in our relationship, we can get through difficult times better. It is inevitable that we will experience some stormy times with our children as it is part of the journey of parenthood. For example, when we have to travel leaving a child behind, when there is a distressing situation in the family or even when there is a new sibling at home—connection is the only thing that becomes our saviour at that time and helps us bounce back to happier times sooner.

2.   Connection helps in our children's brain development

When we establish a strong connection with our children, we help their brains to develop in a healthy way. The neurons in children's brains are firing every second and forming their own connections based on the experiences that they are having with different people. Every interaction a child has develops their brain by establishing neural connections, which in turn form a sort of blueprint that they will use in the future to make sense of the world and others as they grow up.

When we consciously work on building connections with our children, they grow up feeling more secure and accepted—the healthy neural connections in their brains help them to become more confident human beings capable of forming more fulfilling and connected relationships in their lives. It also helps them in becoming more emotionally intelligent and resilient when they grow up.

Connection is a fundamental need of a child when they are born. That is why, if we fail to form a connection, we see more tantrums in our children as tantrums are a way in which our children communicate that they are feeling disconnected and need our attention.

3.   The relationship becomes beautiful and genuine

Connection is the essence of any relationship. When we genuinely invest in connecting with our children, it makes parenting much more fulfilling and beautiful.

These are some of the changes you will see when you have a strong connection with your child:

- There is more acceptance of each other, and fewer complaints and comparisons.
- There is more cooperation with each other, and less manipulation and threats.
- There are more respectful boundaries, and less anger and punishments.
- There is more compassion and understanding, and fewer arguments and blame games.

Conclusion

To deal with any parenting challenge in our lives, we need to have a connection. Remember, we cannot control our children's behaviour, but when we connect with them, we get more influence over their decisions.

We do have to make rules and set boundaries for our children as it is part of being a parent. But when we simultaneously work on establishing a strong connection, it saves us from being the bad guy despite being the rule-maker and we get more cooperation from our children in following the rules we put in place. (We will learn more about making rules and boundaries in the discipline section.)

At the end of this section, I want to reiterate that *connection is the base of parenting*; in fact, it is the base of any relationship. Sometimes we are so busy raising our children that, in that process, we forget to connect with them.

Remember, the relationship we share with our kids does not exist only for the duration of the time that they are growing. Once children become adults, our relationship with them becomes an adult-to-adult relationship, which lasts for the rest of our lives. What our relationship with them will be like at that time has a lot to do with how we interacted with our children when they were little. So, invest in your connection with your child and it will take you a long way as a parent.

III

CALM PARENTING

8

Is Calm Parenting Really Effective?

'My child does not listen to me when I am calm,
I have to get angry.'
'If I stay calm, my child will learn to take me
for granted.'
'I try to be calm but I lose it in the moment and
regret it later.'
'It is not possible to be calm all the time!'
'If I always stay calm, how will my child learn to
face the harshness of the real world?'

In my experience, most parents find it difficult to understand and believe that calm parenting can be effective. A common question they have is: 'How can we make children listen to us without showing our authority by being angry?' When we are looking for parenting advice and someone tells us to be calm, we lose interest in the advice almost instantly. We often feel that calm parenting will not work and sounds good in theory, whereas, in practice, it falls apart. We may also believe we don't have the confidence to be calm through challenging situations on a regular basis, and thus, trying to be a calm parent is sure to result in failure. These doubts and insecurities are only natural—when I began my journey of being a calm parent, I had these same reservations.

The truth is that the parenting strategy of being calm is extremely underrated but also very powerful. In this section, I will not only explain to you the benefits of being calm but also share with you practical ways in which we can start the journey towards being calm parents.

But first, let us understand what happens when we are not calm while parenting our children in different situations. How does that play out in our children's growth and our relationship with them? And let's see if not being calm is helping us at all in reaching our parenting goals.

If we make a conscious effort to observe our behaviour when we are not calm in our interactions with our children, we will realize that we are either showing anger towards them or being anxious around them. There may be a variety of emotions we feel in a negative moment, but here, I am classifying them into two broad categories to make it easier to analyse them and effectively reflect.

1. What happens when we get angry?

'I must get angry to get things done by my child or else, my child does not listen to me. Anger is what gets me results.'

One of the reasons we are so motivated to use anger with our children is that we perceive that this emotion seems to get us the results we want in situations where we need our children's cooperation. When we raise our voices to shout at and threaten them, our children finally do what we are asking them to do. Soon, it starts looking like the only way to get things done and becomes an effective quick-fix parenting solution.

If we think about it, no one plans to act like angry parents when their children are born. In the first few months of a baby's life, there is no need to discipline them as they are hardly doing anything. It is when our little babies are around a year old that they start moving and exploring their environments for the first time and we start facing situations where we have to limit their actions, such as stopping them from touching something harmful or going somewhere undesirable. It is in these situations, when our little children show resistance and refuse to follow our instructions, that we almost automatically raise our voices and say, 'DON'T TOUCH THAT' or 'DON'T GO OVER THERE, LISTEN TO ME'.

When we react in this way, we find that, more often than not, the child stops immediately after being alarmed by our tone. It convinces us that this way of talking to the child works in gaining their cooperation. Add to it the fact that most of us were raised in a similar manner as well, and we learnt to believe in the efficacy of anger in achieving desired results from our own childhoods. All this motivates us to raise our voices and show anger every time our children refuse to listen to or cooperate with us.

We don't even realize when, with time, anger becomes a part of our daily interactions with our children. Whenever we need our children to do something and they show resistance, we resort to showing anger. In completing routine tasks like finishing their homework, eating their meal and going to bed, or stopping our children from using a bad word or being aggressive, we start relying on anger to gain their cooperation. And it seems to work for us!

Now, before we go ahead, take a moment to reflect on the following questions:

- Do you think the tasks for which you are using anger with your child are getting easier to complete over time? Or is the child's struggle increasing?
- Whatever behaviour you are trying to correct in your child through anger—is that getting better with time? Or is the child increasingly repeating that behaviour, forcing you to get angry every time to make them listen to you?
- Do you think the intensity of anger that you used to discipline your child in the beginning is still the same? Or has your anger increased with time?

The truth is that anger makes us delusional because it leads us to believe that the emotion is working in our favour when in reality, it is making things worse for us.

Let me show you what anger is really doing to us in the long term:

a. Anger makes our children stubborn and worsens our interactions with them over time

Being angry at the negative behaviours of our children may seem to be effective in resolving them at that moment, but over time, we start noticing that our everyday struggles are increasing around that very behaviour. For example, if we resort to getting angry to make our child sit down to study, we will find that they are becoming more stubborn and throwing more tantrums every time they have to study so that they can avoid it. Anything to do with studies brings in a lot of negative associations, which in turn makes this activity increasingly challenging with every passing day. The same applies to children in terms of eating or finishing their food, getting up in the morning for school and so on.

Another effect that anger has when indulged in regularly, is that the intensity we feel keeps increasing with time. As our children get used to our outbursts, they become immune to our anger. As a result, we find ourselves needing to increase the level of anger in similar situations over time to make our children pay any heed to us. We may have to raise our voices, make our words and threats more serious, or even try to look more ferocious to make our children take us seriously and cooperate. These may work in a few instances before the effect is lost and we have to increase the intensity of our anger further.

Can you see the vicious cycle we are getting stuck in? Our children keep becoming immune to our anger and we keep getting worse in our behaviour to get them to cooperate.

b. Anger only works till the time the child allows it to work

Even if children do seem to cooperate when we get angry with them, if they decide, 'I am not going to listen and do what my parents say even if they get angry', there is nothing much we can do. At some point, our anger completely stops getting the desired results and our child may refuse to cooperate with us in spite of the anger we direct at them.

At times like these, we might feel so frustrated and helpless that it may lead us to raise our hand on our child or at least feel the instinct to do so. Most parents do not ever want to hit their children, but they end up doing it anyway because they see no other way to make their children listen to them. They feel that no other option remains as they still have to get things done, and this is when their frustration takes over. But, meting out corporal punishment is a very unhelpful way to get children to cooperate and its effects are, at best, temporary. As discussed in the earlier section of this book, we cannot control our children's behaviour. We only believe that we can because anger seems to work in some situations for gaining a useful response from our children, but it does backfire at some point. When that point is reached, varies from child to child. For my strong-willed son, this point came sooner rather than later when he started retaliating to my anger in his first few years. For some parents, this point comes when children are older or perhaps when they reach adolescence.

Anger is just a temporary fix for our problems; only a connection with our children brings us their true cooperation and gives us lasting influence over them. Anger, in fact, ruins the connection. When trying to break our habit of lapsing into anger, it may be helpful to remind ourselves that we *cannot* control our children's behaviour but we *can* control our own behaviour. It is important that we focus on that.

c. Anger may make children submissive and quiet, and kill their true spirit in the process

Depending on their temperament, some children do not rebel against our anger but shut down. When we meet these children, they may seem to be very well-behaved, making us believe that the anger is working well in disciplining them, while in reality, the child is suppressing their emotions because they are not getting the space to express themselves. With time, these children start showing signs of low confidence or insecurity and become more withdrawn or irritable as they feel invalidated and disconnected. What is more alarming is that because these children suppress their feelings, their emotions do not find a healthy outlet and come to the surface in a distorted manner as they grow. This might lead to mental health issues, some of which could take the rest of their lives to overcome.

d. Anger teaches our children to get angry at others
   Have you ever seen your child get angry just like you do? Using the same enraged gestures, words and tones? Children observe and learn from our behaviour constantly. When we get angry because we are upset, children learn the wrong lesson: 'When things do not go according to my mom or dad, they get angry and start shouting, and that is okay. So, next time when things don't go as I want them to, I will start shouting too.' This is what we are unconsciously teaching our children when we fail to regulate ourselves around them. It is difficult for children to learn to regulate their behaviour and understand their emotions if they are constantly experiencing parental anger and growing up in such an environment. This may even have long-term effects on our children's lives in their future relationships—personal and professional.

e. Anger makes us guilty and unhappy parents
   As a parent, I can vouch for the fact that we definitely do not enjoy getting angry at our kids. How many times have you regretted shouting at your child and gone to bed feeling guilty? Getting

angry with our children on a regular basis not only takes a toll on our children's mental health but affects our own mental well-being as well. It strains our relationship with our children and makes parenting stressful as our connection with them is lost or weak. Somewhere in our hearts, we know that the anger we express is negatively affecting our child and our relationship, which adds to our guilt and stress.

2. **What happens when we get anxious instead of regulating our emotions around our child?**

Sometimes, we get anxious when situations with our children become strained (please note that I am not talking about strictly clinical anxiety here). We may not be shouting at our child at that moment, but we are not calm in our minds and bodies either. We become too worried or nervous instead. Feeling anxious in difficult situations is normal and we all feel this emotion at some time or the other. But when we do not handle this emotion in the right way and constantly get agitated around our children, the following is how matters play out:

a. The child becomes dysregulated: When we regularly lose our calm and get too anxious around our children, they catch on to our state of mind. They too become dysregulated and are unable to cooperate with us or behave better in the situation.

When we are constantly anxious, we will see more tantrums in our children as well. This happens because, firstly, they are not witnessing an adult regulating their behaviour and learning from them, and so are unable to learn regulation themselves. Secondly, children look to us adults for safety and when the parent gets too anxious in a situation, children feel unsafe, like something is not right, and it affects their behaviour even if they do not understand what is happening.

b. A child who has anxious parents may develop anxiety themselves in the long run: When we are unable to cope with situations in healthy ways, our children are unable to learn this invaluable skill themselves. Children automatically adopt the same way of dealing with similar situations as their parents. For example, if a parent gets very tense during their child's exams, as the child grows up, they will also take a lot of exam stress despite being good at studies. If you as a parent feel that you are unable to control your anxiety in different situations, it may be worthwhile to recall if your parents had anxiety when you were a child—you may find that you have picked up the tendency of being anxious from them.

c. The child starts suppressing emotions so that they don't make the parent too anxious: Some children start to suppress their emotions and hide things from their parents, just to avoid making their parent too anxious. They feel that the parent may not be able to handle the stress. Remember, we can only be helpful and approachable to our children if we are in a state of calm.

I hope this information helps you assess your own situation with your child in a better light and motivates you towards the first steps of being a 'calm parent'.

Why does 'being calm' not work in some situations?

'Even when I don't get angry and stay calm, my child still does not listen to me.'

Many parents want to be calm parents but then give up along the way, because it does not seem to be working for them. Here, I want to lay down the most common reasons why being calm does not work:

1. Most parents are not really calm, they are just quiet

Being calm does not mean being quiet or not shouting. This is a common misconception that most parents have—they assume that if they are not saying anything, they are being calm. But if our thoughts are racing and our body is strained, then we are not exactly calm, are we?

What do we mean when we say 'be calm'? To understand this, we need to become more conscious of how we are feeling in our mind and body. In any difficult situation, ask yourself the following questions:

- How am I feeling physically?
  a. Is my heart racing?
  b. Is my body strained or stiff in different areas?
  c. Is my body vibrating from inside?
  d. Is my breathing fast and shallow?
- How am I feeling in my mind?
  a. Are my thoughts racing?
  b. Are my thoughts negative?
  c. Am I feeling unsafe in my head?
  d. Is my mind not clear? Am I not able to catch up with my own thoughts?

These answers will help you realize if you really are calm or if you are just pretending to be or thinking you are.

When you start becoming more conscious of how you feel in your body in challenging moments, you start to understand how a calm body feels more comfortable and in control, and how a restless body feels strained and out of control. When you consciously take a deep breath, you may realize how shallow your breathing was till then. If you just take five deep and long breaths right now while paying attention to your breathing alone, you will feel a change in your body. You may just experience a sense of 'calm'. (Do try this right now if you never have.)

Most of us go through our daily lives in such a mechanical manner, unconscious of how we are really feeling in our body and mind, that we do not even know what a calm state looks and feels like. We need to start observing ourselves and watch our tone, expressions and body language as these give us many clues about our state of mind and help us figure out if we are actually calm from the inside. Remember, even if we are quiet, the rest of our behaviour is communicating a lot to our child. I want to share my own experience here as an example:

When the COVID-19 lockdown was in effect in India in 2020, Saiveer was three and a half years old. Almost everything, including his schooling, had shifted online. My son had to attend online classes, but at that age, it was extremely difficult for him to sit in one place for that long when attending the lessons, let alone focus and learn from them. He was a very energetic child and his way of learning was more through play, manipulation and movement. Thus, it became very challenging for me to make him sit in front of a laptop every day for two to three hours for his classes.

I used many strategies to help him sit and focus. I even allowed him to move around in the room every fifteen minutes so that he could move his body and therefore, concentrate better. But nothing seemed to work. I felt demotivated as he was not cooperating with me, and the situation was getting worse. After trying everything I could think of for a week, one day, I decided to take a backseat. I planned on doing nothing and expecting nothing but simply sitting beside my son and letting him be the way he wanted to be while his classes went on. I just sat calmly, breathing and observing. To my surprise, that day turned out to be much better than so many other days had been.

When I reflected on what had really worked this time, I realized that I had been very anxious in the classes with my son till then. I was unknowingly getting stressed looking at the other children in his class, who seemed to be sitting so calmly through the online classes, and my body was giving away the fact that I was anxious about my child not coping as well as his classmates were.

After that day, keeping my body calm became my priority no matter how my son was behaving during class. I remember repeating a few affirmations to myself before his classes to help me maintain my calm. To my surprise, my son started cooperating more and more with me as the days passed. He still found it challenging to sit and focus for long durations, but keeping myself calm, taking one day at a time and keeping my expectations of him realistic helped a lot in overcoming the challenges.

Our anxiety really does pass on to our children, and so does our calmness. This above experience reinforced this fact for me. So, in difficult situations, try to pause, breathe, observe your body instead of reacting, and see for yourself how that situation turns out differently.

2. Children get used to only listening to your angry tone

Sometimes, anger becomes such a pattern of communication with our children that they literally wait for us to shout before they respond to us as they are not used to paying heed to our calm voice.

Many a time, parents say, 'I try to be calm, but when it does not work, I end up losing it'. After trying to be calm at the beginning of a situation, if you end up angry, then that is not an effective scenario—the pattern of responding only to anger is still intact and your child is still waiting for you to lose it.

For your child to get used to a new pattern, they need to repeatedly see it taking place. You will have to learn to be calm and get through situations without giving in to your anger while maintaining all the boundaries you have set in place. You will have to be consistent in your behaviour to build a new way of communication with your children. (We will talk about how to maintain boundaries while being calm in the discipline section.)

3. There is an existing disconnection in the relationship already

A lot depends not only on how we are dealing with our child in a particular moment but also on how our relationship with them is in general. If we try to be calm in isolated instances but get irritated and lose our patience in our day-to-day interactions, then being calm in a challenging situation now and again may not bring us the desired behavioural change.

If there is an existing disconnection, then we first need to work on the overall relationship by examining and fixing any communication gaps that may crop up. We need to check for factors such as, 'Am I correcting my child too much?', 'Am I getting angry and irritated with my child a lot?', 'Are my expectations from my child realistic?' and so on.

We have discussed all these points in detail in the previous section and I hope you have picked up effective strategies from there. Sometimes, relationships get so strained due to continuous negative interactions from certain harmful patterns that being calm in isolated situations is not enough, though it may still be an important first step towards making a change. So, do not lose hope; work on building your connection with your child while working on your own regulation and see the result for yourself.

How Does Being Calm Help Us?

'What happens when I start practising being calmer while dealing with my child?'

1. The child learns to regulate their behaviour better as they grow. They learn healthy ways to cope with their emotions.

When we are calm, it does not mean that we are not feeling any emotions. Instead, we are working on regulating ourselves and our behaviour despite the (negative) emotions that we are experiencing. When we model this skill of self-regulation to our children, they automatically learn it from us as they grow.

As I keep stressing, children are learning from us every day just by observing us. If we get angry and threaten a lot, argue or blame others often, then no matter how we behave with or around our children, over time, they will pick up our negative traits and show the same kind of behaviour and coping mechanisms.

Children see and learn from what we do when we experience different emotions ourselves. How do we cope with our own feelings? How do we react when things do not go how we want them to? What is our level of tolerance for negative situations? How we parents conduct ourselves has a huge impact on our children's attitudes. It is very difficult for children to learn to regulate themselves if they do not witness adults regulating their behaviour around them.

When we work on our ability to be calm, when we breathe and allow ourselves to feel our emotions instead of shouting and getting irritated with others around us, we model better ways for our children to learn as well. However, do remember that this is not a process that shows quick results—it does take time for children to show these changes in their behaviour as their brains are still developing, so, we need to be more patient with them.

2. When we are calm, we make better decisions and fewer mistakes.

When we are worried, anxious or angry, our mind is overwhelmed with emotions. In such a state, it is not possible for us to think of the right words or solutions in a problematic situation. Our mind literally gets blocked (very much like a child's mind that is unable to access logic during tantrums). At such times, we are unable to think logically or see things from the right perspective. We tend to make more mistakes, speak the wrong words, use the wrong gestures and end up regretting our behaviour later. Instead of helping the child in a difficult moment, we become part of the problem and end up escalating the whole episode.

Now, if in the same situation, we pause for a couple of minutes and breathe to calm our body, it does not only help us to feel better but also, to choose better, and reach a more helpful and appropriate response in the same situation. Only a calm mind can access solution-based thinking. Thus, working on being calm saves us from a lot of damage that we may cause through our own behaviour.

Once we become conscious of ourselves and our emotional states, we are able to recognize when we are not calm. In such situations, it is better to not make important decisions. Instead, it is better to first calm our bodies, let emotions pass and then make decisions, and thus, have fewer regrets. Being calm does not only help us with our children but also helps us in our lives in general.

3. Our connection remains intact and so does our influence over our children.

When we constantly lose control over our own behaviours and get irritated, angry or anxious with our children, it causes a disconnect in our relationship with them. As discussed in the last section, a connection is what gives us more influence over our children's decisions and their behaviour, for we cannot control them.

We think that when we say 'no' to our children and put rules and boundaries in place, it disconnects us from them. But, it is not the rules and boundaries that cause negativity in the parent–child relationship; it has more to do with how we are putting the boundary in place. Are we setting boundaries with anger and condescension or are we being calm and firm while maintaining a respectful tone with them? When we follow the latter method, our relationship with our children does not get as strained.

Setting and following boundaries in a calm way without losing our cool with our child can be very empowering for us as parents. But it is not an easy task, because children are most likely to express their unhappiness at being told 'no' through their behaviour and may also throw a tantrum. For example, when we take back the screen our child may have been playing with, they may show anger and resistance. But once we deal with the tantrum in a calm way (as discussed in the first section of the book), we will see the difference in our future interactions with them. There will be less negativity and the connection will still stay intact.

4. When our body is calm, it radiates the right energy for the child to feel secure in the situation.

Our body is made up of energy. When we are anxious, our body radiates anxious energy, which then passes on to our children. We may not realize this as we cannot see the energy vibrations but know that it affects the child's behaviour. This is the reason why, when we are not calm ourselves, our children are also unable to regulate themselves, making the situation more difficult for both the child and the parent.

It may be hard for you to comprehend this as we cannot see energy, but that does not mean that it does not exist. And our children are definitely very sensitive to the energy that we project. In fact, if you are likely to describe yourself as an anxious or angry parent, then this may be a big reason behind your child's increasing tantrums and decreasing cooperation.

My suggestion is to observe and experiment with this: When you consciously work on maintaining a calm mind and body in a situation by pausing, breathing and observing (in spite of your child's behaviour), see how the conditions change or at the least, do not get worse for you. We will talk more about how to work on calming ourselves down in the last chapter of this section.

9

What Is Stopping Us from Being Calm Parents?

After reading the previous chapter, you may be motivated to be calm while dealing with your children. You may even already be trying to change your pattern of communication. But, many of you will realize at this point that it is not easy to break our old patterns and be calm.

In this chapter, I want to help you reflect on what could be interfering with your decision to stay calm. Let's try to work out why you may still be losing patience and getting angry or anxious around your children. Here is some information that may help you understand yourself better.

1. Our thoughts may be making us agitated

Most of us are always thinking about something or the other in our minds. Though we are not used to considering it, there is a lot of power in the thoughts we choose to think in our minds. Let us understand the nature of this power in two ways.

a. Our thoughts lead us to feel angry or anxious with our children:

The cognitive model used in *Cognitive Behavioural Therapy* by Aaron T. Beck demonstrates that it is not a situation that makes us feel angry or anxious; it is what we *think* about the situation that causes those feelings.[1] This is what the sequence of events looks like:

Situation → Thoughts → Feeling in the body → Behaviour

Let us understand how this works in parenting with the following example:

Two children are playing together in a playground and their parents are sitting on a bench nearby. When it is time to leave, both children start throwing tantrums as they do not want to go home and want to continue playing, which is not possible. Both children begin to argue with their parents and start to cry loudly. One parent gets furious at her child and starts scolding her for being stubborn. The other parent calmly deals with her child and lets the tantrum pass. Both leave the park.

Here, both parents were facing the same challenge, but their way of handling the situation was completely different. This is because each parent was thinking differently at that moment.

The furious parent may have had thoughts like the following:

'Why is my child doing this to me?'

'Even after giving so much time to play, I get this behaviour.'

'What will other people in the part think of my parenting if my child behaves like this?'

'My child is taking advantage of my being calm, I need to shout to get my point across.'

The calm parent may have had thoughts such as:

'My child is having a hard time dealing with his emotions, he is not doing anything to me.'

'My child needs my help to deal with his emotions as his brain is still developing.'

'I am the adult in the situation, I can only help if I approach my child from a place of calm. I need to breathe and not overreact.'

These two different patterns of thinking generated different kinds of emotions in the parents, leading to different responses from each parent towards their child.

It is time to pause and reflect on what we are thinking. When we start thinking too negatively about our children or difficult situations, we end up feeling angry or anxious and tend to get more irritable with our kids. However, now that we know this, we can use this information to reflect on our thought patterns and their relation to our reactions in our everyday situations.

Here are some thoughts that you can consciously harbour in your mind by pausing when involved in a challenging situation with your child, to help you control your reaction and stay calm:

Not every behaviour that my child indulges in reflects my parenting. My child's brain is still in the making and some of the behaviour may be irrational because my child is unable to regulate his or her emotions at this age and needs my help. I can only help them if I approach the situation from a place of calm as I am the adult here. Let me breathe as I am feeling too overwhelmed because of my own triggers.

b. Our thoughts become our reality: Our thoughts create an energy that we give out and ultimately, that is what is manifested in our lives. Delving deeper into this topic is not within the scope of this book but I want to open your minds to this universal truth. The popular author Rhonda Byrne in her book *The Secret* explains the power of thoughts and how the law of attraction works. She emphasizes how what we think, forms our reality.[2] Negative thoughts attract the negative, and positive thoughts have the power to transform our lives in positive ways. Louise Hay in her book, *You Can Heal Your Life*, also emphasizes how our mind has the power to create and affect our future, and when we understand this, we can use that knowledge to turn our lives around.[3] I suggest you read Byrne's and Hay's books to understand this in more detail if this interests you.

Our mind is a machine that is working constantly; we are *always* thinking about something. Many times, we are unaware of what we are thinking. Imagine yourself brushing your teeth, taking a bath, cooking in the kitchen or working on the laptop: you are doing the task at hand, but the task is so automated that you are hardly fully mentally present and engaged at that moment in that task. Instead, your mind is simultaneously thinking about something else while your body completes the mundane tasks mechanically.

Often, our minds are conditioned to think in certain ways due to our experiences from childhood onwards, and that may be getting in our way. For example, we may tend to focus on the negatives more than the positives in any situation or tend to judge people in different ways. It is important for us to identify unhealthy thought patterns and consciously break from them to better our quality of life. And with that, we must learn to consciously practise healthier ways of thinking. It may not always be easy to break these patterns that we have developed over the years, and we may need the help of tools such as practising mindfulness or meditation techniques. We may even require help from professionals (such as therapists) to understand ourselves and identify the thought patterns that may not be working for us or holding us back.

Remember that whenever we feel an emotion, it is caused by our underlying thoughts. Know that it is easier to identify what we are feeling than figure out what exactly we are thinking that is giving rise to specific feelings. For example, we may feel sad or upset but not understand why we are feeling these emotions at a particular moment.

At times, we are not even aware of our feelings, but our behaviour and reactions to others show us that something is going on in our minds. For example, when I start losing patience with my son, I pause and reflect on what is happening inside me, what am I feeling and thinking? More often than not, I find I am upset or agitated without even being conscious of it and these negative emotions translate into negative responses towards others.

In conclusion, we must remember that if we want to undertake the journey of becoming a calm parent, it is important that we become more conscious and watch our thoughts. They have the power to change our state of mind and help us be calmer.

I hope this information and understanding will help you in taking the first steps towards more conscious living.

2. Worried parents end up being anxious/angry parents

As parents, it is natural to be concerned about our children. We may worry about their physical and mental development, their behaviour and their habits. The emotion of worry is helpful in ways that it alerts us to the possibility of there being something we need to pay attention to and work on with our children. For example, a child who is not speaking even at the age

of two and a half years may need a speech therapist, and only the feeling of worry will make the parent take action towards helping the child. If we do not feel any emotion, how will the child get the intervention he or she needs?

But when we let worry take over our minds, it causes more problems. Firstly, it does not let us formulate any solutions because our minds are too busy worrying and we are too agitated to take the right actions to meet our own goals. (Remember, only a calm mind can achieve solution-based thinking.)

Secondly, when we get overly worried, it affects our behaviour. We tend to become angry and anxious in the situation, aggravating the problem instead of solving it. I will share my own experience here.

My son loved to write but he did not enjoy writing within the lines. His letter formations would go out of the lines, making his writing look very clumsy and untidy. I could see that other children of the same age as him were writing beautifully within the lines and naturally, this 'lack' in my son worried me. I remember when I received a note from his teacher that asked me to help my son practise writing within the lines, my worry skyrocketed. Panic overtook me and I started to correct my son too much whenever he practised his writing skills. My tone and behaviour would get anxious and I would say things like, 'You are not writing well' and 'Look at that formation, write it again', and I would get more and more impatient. Within a couple of days, I saw my son lose interest in writing. He stopped practising forming letters altogether and especially avoided writing whenever I was around. Thankfully, I observed this sooner rather than later. I worked on my thoughts of worry, identifying the stress I was causing my child during the process of writing. I worked on calming myself down and controlling my behaviour. I trained my mind to make peace with the fact that 'not all children can write the same'.

This helped me gain my child's interest back in the activity, even though he was still not forming his letters in an ideal manner. I even found effective ways of encouraging him to write better without making the activity stressful for him.

In the situation I just described, if I had not changed my thoughts and approach, I would have caused my son to completely lose interest and confidence in writing. My worry that his skills were not improving would have become the barrier in his writing, instead of actually making the situation better.

You can apply the lessons from this experience in whichever situation your child struggles with— speaking and greeting people, reading, dancing. Observe how you are dealing with your child when it comes to reacting to the behaviour that worries you because your response matters more than the child's behaviour. **If there is stress attached to any activity that you engage in with your child, it will interfere with the process of learning for them.**

If you are a parent who worries a lot about your child, then it is going to be very difficult for you to be calm around them. A parent who has a tendency to worry will find something or the other to worry about at all times. Some of us are so prone to worrying that we may start worrying about our 'too much worrying' right now!

Sometimes, our worry is not even rational. We need to objectively consider how much we worry about every behaviour and milestone of our children. For instance, we do not need to worry about an eighteen-month-old not speaking, a three-year-old not writing or a two-year-old experimenting with hitting or not sitting in one place. It will be helpful for every parent to refer to physical and behavioural milestone charts for children so that they know if whatever they are worried about in their child is actually normal and to be expected.

Another thing a worried parent tends to do is discuss their worries with other people around their children. And as we have read earlier, it is not good for our children to overhear us talking about them in this way. First, this makes them think that there is something wrong with them. Second, they start losing confidence. And third, they do not feel motivated to improve as they accept that this is the way they are.

Imagine a child who did not start speaking even at the age of two and requires some intervention and support from a speech therapist. The parent gets so worried about the child not speaking that he or she keeps discussing this concern with family members, the paediatrician and the child's school teachers, all while the child is around. Here, more than the delay in the child's speech, I would be concerned about what the child is hearing about themselves from the parents. Ultimately, the child may start speaking clearly within a few months, but in that process, they may start showing behaviours of low confidence and low self-esteem.

If you feel you are struggling to be a calm parent, then you need to see if you are a worried parent, reflect on what is making you worried and work on dealing with the emotion in a better way.

3. Fear of being too lenient or spoiling our child

'If I am always calm with my child, I am afraid that it will make me lenient and my child will take me for granted.'

This is the most common misconception that we have that stops us from being calmer parents. We assume that if we are not angry or not raising our voices, our children will stop listening to us completely or take us for granted, and we will fall into the category of parents who do not set boundaries for their children. Let us clarify how this is the wrong way of looking at things.

Firstly, while being calm parents, we still must set firm boundaries for our children. When we do not have clear boundaries, it is difficult for children to understand what are appropriate and inappropriate behaviours as they grow. This leads them to become more and more dysregulated. It is not when the parent is calm that the child's behaviour becomes difficult. The child's difficult behaviour starts when we:

- give in to their demands due to tantrums;
- offer empty threats and do not follow through with our words;
- get irritated and dysregulated in the situation ourselves; and
- fail to stick to our 'no' or do not have consistent boundaries.

All this confuses our children and leads to more stubbornness, tantrums and lack of control in their behaviour.

A child needs clear and firm boundaries to aid their healthy brain development. A child who is not used to rules and boundaries will not know how to follow them even when they grow up. (But, of course, we need to keep our expectations realistic while forming these boundaries for our children: they must be age-appropriate and reasonable. We will discuss this in the next section.)

When we follow being a calm parent, the way in which we set boundaries tends to look different. We practise being firm instead of being angry when required, and the huge difference between the two can be perceived in the tone in which we choose to speak, in the words we use and in our body language. When we are firm, we are in control of our emotions and can be kind while still maintaining clear boundaries. On the other hand, when we are angry, we let our emotions come in the way of discipline and often lose control over ourselves and our words. Also, when we are firm, our body is calm from the inside and our tone is confident and matter-of-fact, which is not the case when we are angry or even anxious.

Let's see how our words are different when we are angry and when we are firm.

Angry	Calm and firm
'How can you do this?'	'We don't do this.'
'You always start crying when I say no to TV; I am so tired of this.'	'I can see this made you upset, but we still can't watch TV before going to bed.'
'I have told you many times, this cup can break easily. I cannot give it to you. Why don't you understand?'	'You like the red colour of this cup. I know you do. But we cannot play with it, even if we cry, as it can break easily. I am sorry.'
'Enough is enough. If you don't sit down to study right now, I won't give you any screen time today!'	'We will do our work now. If we don't complete this, I will not be able to give you the screen, and I really do want you to watch and not miss your favourite shows. I know you can do this.'

As you can see from this, being calm definitely does not mean pampering our children all the way or giving in to their demands. (How we maintain the boundaries we have set and discipline our children when required is discussed in the following sections of the book.)

When we are calm while setting a boundary in place, we are in control of our inner mental environment, which in turn helps us control the outer physical situation more effectively. As parents, we are the authority for our children, considering we are the ones forming their routines and giving them permission to do different things. When our children see the authority figures in their lives (us) lose control over themselves, it gets difficult for them to take us seriously.

When we get intimidated because of our children's crying, anger or rudeness and it makes us lose control over our behaviour, we transfer control of the situation to the child and give power to their negative behaviour. This can obviously lead to their bad behaviour getting stronger and worse.

Remember: Being calm is our power. It allows us to control our own state of mind and does not make us try to control others. Sometimes, in trying to control our children's behaviour, which we have seen we can't do, we lose our grip over our own behaviour, something we can control. It is consequently extremely important to start putting more effort into regulating ourselves before trying to manage our child's behaviour.

4. A guilty parent cannot be a calm parent*

We all feel guilty as parents at some time or the other. It is as if when we become a parent, the feeling of guilt comes as a package deal. However, it is important to

---

* These thoughts are inspired by Aaron Beck's *Cognitive Behaviour Therapy* and Louise Hay's *You Can Heal Your Life*. You can delve deeper into these books if the issue resonates with you.

learn to deal with this feeling in healthy ways, understand what we can do, make our peace with what we cannot and remember that we will make mistakes too and thus, learn to love and forgive ourselves in the process.

Guilty parents tend to be very hard on themselves. When we feel guilty, we are unable to forgive ourselves for our deficiencies and mistakes, and start imposing too many 'shoulds' on ourselves.

'I should not have shouted at my child; I should have controlled myself.'

'I should always be able to solve my child's problems.'

'I should be able to stay calm with my child always.'

'I should give time to my child.'

When we are unable to do what we think we *should* do, we become extremely uncomfortable and guilty, making our behaviour more reactive with our children.

Like worry, guilt also has a purpose in our lives. It helps us work on ourselves and be better parents. But when we do not deal with it effectively, we get stuck in a cycle where feeling guilty makes us feel worse, which leads us to behave in worse ways with our kids, leading to further guilt. A guilty parent tends to become an angry or anxious parent.

Another point worth noticing here is that when we are too hard on ourselves, we automatically become hard on our children too. Just as we are unable to accept our mistakes, we are unable to forgive our children's mistakes as well. We start expecting a lot of 'shoulds' with our children too.

Expectations from ourselves	Expectations from our children
'I should be polite to my elders.'	*'My child should be polite to his elders.'*
'I should never make a mistake.'	*'My child should never make a mistake.'*
'I should always be calm.'	*'My child should always be calm.'*

There is nothing wrong with these values, but ask yourself: Can anyone be perfect all the time? Are we expecting that we will never make mistakes and that our children, in the process of growing up, will never mess up? Do we need to be hard on ourselves or our children for making mistakes? In fact, should we not see mistakes as opportunities to learn? When we recognize this and accordingly change our thoughts regarding our mistakes, it can help us love and accept ourselves and our children more. Here are some ways we can work on our thought processes:

Realistic expectations from ourselves	Realistic expectations from our children
'I wanted to be polite but I got triggered and lost my cool. But that does not mean I am a bad human being.'	*'I wish my child to be polite but he messed up, that does not mean he/she is not a good child.'*
'I made a mistake, but that does not mean I am good for nothing.'	*'My child made a mistake; it does not make everything my child does wrong.'*

| 'I wanted to stay calm but I lost it; that does not mean I am a bad parent.' | 'My child got too angry, he couldn't help it; he has a beautiful heart, though.' |

When we think like this, it helps us feel better and allows us to effectively work on making things right instead of making them worse. Guilt is the enemy of being calm; self-love and self-acceptance are the right paths that lead towards calm parenting, and towards loving and accepting our children unconditionally too.

5. We are tired, exhausted and stressed out

Along with our duties of parenthood, we are dealing with challenges in different areas of life as well, like our relationships, our physical and mental health, our financial strains and so much more. When we are mentally or physically exhausted or stressed out, we become the most vulnerable to losing our calm. We may use the wrong words, overreact or behave in ways that we may regret later.

I understand that we are human beings and cannot be perfectly calm all the time, especially in challenging situations. But can we be more mindful of our behaviour? I think, yes. Remember, our behaviour has a strong influence on our children's behaviour. When we are unable to regulate our behaviour with our children, difficult situations become worse for us, because then, our children also start reacting by being more stubborn, throwing more tantrums and not listening to us. Here, we unknowingly add to our existing problem, as now the child also becomes the source of stress. We may even think, 'I have already been going through so much, and now my child is also giving me such a hard time', without realizing that our own behaviour may be causing the complications.

So, it is all the more important that we become more conscious about our feelings and start pausing in situations instead of reacting emotionally when we are agitated, so as to save ourselves from our own behaviour. Remember, once we have uttered something, we cannot take it back. Even a fifteen-second pause when we are feeling anxious or agitated may sometimes change the words we choose to use if we become more mindful of how we are really feeling. We will talk more about this technique of regulating ourselves in the next chapter.

I want to re-emphasize here, that parents who don't take care of their mental and physical health tend to lose their calm and become irritated around their children more often. It is extremely important for us parents to take care of and prioritize ourselves while providing for our children and our families. 'We can't pour from an empty cup'—we tend to forget this when we become parents as our children become our biggest priority and we start to ignore our responsibility of looking after ourselves while taking care of them.

Also, in many cultures, parents—especially mothers—sacrificing their own needs in order to devote more time to their children is a kind of behaviour that is promoted as a virtue and considered as being a 'good parent'. In fact, when parents do prioritize themselves, they are often judged for it—somehow, culturally, we have arrived at the conclusion that any time a parent devotes to themselves could be better used by spending it on taking care of the child. But we need to remind ourselves that 'we can only take care of others better when we take care of ourselves'.

I also understand that it may be really difficult for parents to find time for themselves. When I tell parents to take care of themselves, the response I get most often is, 'How can I? I don't have the time.' So, I want to mention here some practical tips that I share with my clients that may help you too. These are ways to include self-care in your routine. It may not equal the luxury of taking a long spa day, but these techniques will help you find pockets of time in the day when you can recharge yourself.

1. Rest when your child is sleeping or enjoying screen time, especially if you can't find any other time in the day to yourself. You can choose to do nothing and give your mind and body a break instead of using that time to finish any pending chore or work.

2. If your spouse or any other family member is available to spend time with the child, plan a peaceful cup of tea for yourself during that break and give yourself those thirty minutes of uninterrupted teatime. Add this to your routine every day. It may make you feel good to just look

forward to that half an hour in the day that you have to yourself.

3. I even suggest that parents take a ten-minute washroom break if they do not seem to find any other time for themselves, and if there are other adults around to look over the child for that duration. When the day gets to be too much, go to the washroom, set a ten-minute alarm, sit back and breathe, come back with a calmer mind, and continue your day.

4. Prioritize your interests and hobbies when you can. Think of what made you happy, what you did to relax, especially before becoming a parent, and invest in those activities. This will help you feel like yourself again, making you a happier and calmer parent.

I understand that every parent's circumstances must be different, involving various challenges when it comes to finding time for themselves. Some may even be doing it all alone, lacking any kind of support in raising their children. But if we can find ways to prioritize ourselves and give ourselves some time in a day, we will be able to make ourselves happy and thus, be calmer parents for our children.

Recognize your triggers

Triggers are behaviours or situations that make us feel intense emotions and may lead to an overreaction from us. We all have different triggers. Each parent gets triggered by different things that their children do.

Some parents may be okay if the child does not study, but when it comes to eating habits, they stress out and get extremely impatient. Similarly, another parent may be okay with their child eating less, but when the child is rude to someone, the parent gets upset, acts irrationally and aggravates the situation instead of handling it in an effective way.

We need to identify our own triggers by watching out for the situations that make us feel anxious. Our triggers may be the result of our childhood experiences, our rigid value systems or our interactions with the people around us. But, one thing is definite: our reactions in situations where we are triggered and agitated are disproportionate and, most often, out of our control.

To illustrate what I mean, let me share the real-life example of a client here:

Reema came to me concerned about her relationship with her six-year-old child, who had started to be rude to her and hide things from her. When we discussed the matter further, she told me that she gets extremely anxious about her child's studies. She gets impatient, shouts a lot and keeps pestering the child to study, even though her child is very good in academics and performs well in every exam.

Reema even confessed to me, 'I know she is doing well, but I do not know what happens to me. I feel she should not face what I had to face.' Then she disclosed

---

* Name changed.

how when she was a child, she fell sick in one semester and started lagging in her class. As a result, she lost her confidence in academics and it became a major source of distress for her. Her mother was also very anxious and the negative association with studies for her started from there. Reema had somehow completed her own phase of studying, which was not easy for her, but now, her anxiety around academic performance was affecting her child. She could see that like her, her child had also developed anxiety around her exams. What was more, this tension was ruining the child's relationship with Reema. I suggested that Reema seek professional help from a therapist to deal with her anxiety so that it does not pass on to her child.

Here's another example from my own life as well:

I was always taught to be an obedient child and took to pleasing everyone. I would try to please my teachers and want to win their hearts by getting more 'stars' in class and performing well in my studies. I really enjoyed their words of praise for me. I never realized how my childhood experiences had made me a 'people pleaser' and become a part of my value system.

Unknowingly, I wanted my son to please others too, which he did not seem to be interested in. I remember, during his online classes when he did not want to raise his hand and answer questions or did not show interest in getting stars, I would get anxious and push him to do these things. I would say, 'Why don't you raise your hand, see everyone is answering so well?' or 'You will not get a star like this, ma'am will not be happy.' My behaviour around his online classes was making my son lose interest in them. He even stopped answering his teacher where he had been occasionally doing so earlier.

I realized how I was pushing my son to be a people pleaser, something he was not. My son's reality in comparison to my expectations was acting as a trigger for me, making me anxious and uncomfortable during the online classes. Recognizing my trigger, consciously working on being calmer and not pushing him during his classes helped a lot in gaining his interest back in the classes.

I started focusing on what made my son happy and comfortable, and I encouraged him in those directions instead of forcing him to do things only to please others. In fact, I learnt from him how NOT to be a people pleaser and still be happy.

There is so much to learn from our children if we are willing to pay attention. Children reveal to us those parts of ourselves that we did not even know existed. They come into our worlds to teach us something and help us evolve as human beings—we only have to open ourselves to learn from them.

10

How to Start the Journey of Being a 'Calm Parent'?

What Is Stopping Us from Being Calm Parents?

When we start walking on the path of being calm parents, it does not mean that we can never get angry, irritated or lose our patience. If we aim to be perfectly calm as soon as we start trying gentle parenting, we will get demotivated and lose hope due to our unrealistic expectations. Becoming calmer is a journey in which, we, as human beings, are bound to experience many different emotions. In fact, in learning to be calmer, we must allow ourselves to feel our emotions and manage them well by finding better ways of handling difficult situations.

Parents invariably have a set pattern of responding to their children in various situations. We get irritated, angry, anxious, argumentative and so on, especially in challenging situations. Whatever response we employ most regularly becomes our automatic response when in a crisis, and we do not have to think twice before reacting in the same way again. Even if we plan to stay calm, we may, at times, lapse into our familiar pattern only to regret our reaction later and feel disheartened by our lack of control.

It is at times like these that we need to be patient with ourselves and remember that, if we consciously work on ourselves and practise helpful ways of handling challenging situations, we will become good at it. When I started working on myself as a parent, I found it extremely difficult to pause and change my response as it required constant effort from me. But with practice, pausing and reflecting started coming more naturally to me. So, even if you lose your calm at some moments during your journey, remember to not lose hope; instead, bounce back and keep working on yourself. Let me help you with some practical steps to begin your journey of being calmer:

1. Start observing your own behaviour

The first step is to start observing your own behaviour patterns without judgement.

How do I respond to my child most of the time?
Is my body calm or am I mostly reacting?
In which situations do I lose my calm with my child?
What behaviours trigger me the most?
Where is the trigger coming from?

Here, the major shift is going to be the focus—instead of complaining about and concentrating on our children's behaviour, we start watching our own behaviour.

This is not an easy process because, when we start introspecting and go on this inner journey, it may get uncomfortable as we face our own deficiencies and unhelpful patterns. Thus, it is very essential for us to be kind and patient with ourselves and accept ourselves without judgement.

The first step is to identify our behavioural patterns and the second is to work on changing them. As mentioned earlier, we will not be able to abruptly start being calmer all the time. We have to be realistic and aim to work on reducing the frequency and intensity of our unwanted behaviours when we are not calm first.

- **Frequency:** Observe how many times in a day you get irritated, angry or anxious. Check if you keep losing your patience repeatedly with your child. Work on reducing the number of instances you become agitated and gradually increase the number of instances you are able to respond calmly. In the beginning, you will be calm only three out of ten times, but with practice, you can increase that number to seven, eight or nine out of ten times.

- **Intensity:** Watch yourself to figure out the extent you lose control over yourself. Are you unable to stop escalating your reactions once you start getting angry? It is important to get back in control as soon as we realize that our behaviour is going in the wrong direction instead of allowing ourselves to be swept away by our negative emotions. You have the power to change your behaviour, even during your reaction, the moment you realize it. You may pause and say something like, 'I am sorry, I don't know why I started shouting like that. Can we not dirty this sweetheart? Else I will not be able to allow you to play with water.'

I remember when I was practising new ways of responding in a calm manner, I would still tend to start with my automatic reaction and realize midway that that reaction was not going to take me anywhere. I would instantly stop and tell my child, 'Darling, I don't know why I am speaking like this. I don't want to speak like this. I think I need to breathe for a second.'

This would not only give me a chance to rectify my response but also help my child observe how I was trying to calm my body and regulate my behaviour. The key is to be realistic and start with small steps when beginning the journey of calm parenting.

2. Start pausing before you react in a situation involving your child

While observing our patterns, we will need to learn to pause before reacting to situations. That is the only way we can break our long-established patterns, overcome any overwhelming emotions and think clearly.

When we pause, we give ourselves a moment to change our reaction into a more helpful response to the situation. If we don't pause, we will end up saying something that will not help us or our child and may even worsen our situation. Pausing helps us to increase the gap between the time we experience our erupting emotions and the time we respond to the situation.

For example, say you got triggered when your three-year-old child threw food on the floor. Your first impulse may be getting angry and shouting at your child for this misbehaviour. At that moment, just pause and do not say anything for thirty seconds. You will see that your reaction may change into a better response, which will actually save you from worsening the situation. Also, what you are doing during the pause is extremely important.

When you pause, do the following:

- Break and change your thought process: Pausing your behaviour without pausing your thoughts will render the break ineffective. In fact, you may end up shouting even more if your thoughts are racing (you may be thinking, 'How can she behave like this? She is disrespecting food!'). Pause your thoughts as well and then perhaps, try to change them into something more helpful. For instance, in the situation we just looked at, you may remind yourself: 'It is just a three-year-old child who is experimenting with different behaviours and if I overreact, it will just increase this behaviour in the future.'

- Breathe and calm your body: One of the most effective ways of taking back control of your mind and thoughts is through conscious breathing in that moment. During the pause, start breathing deeply and focus on your breath so that your mind stops wandering and thinking in unhelpful ways. It will also help you calm your body and let the negative feelings that you are experiencing pass faster.

- Allow yourself to feel your feelings: When we pause, we do not suppress our emotions. If you do that, then you will experience an outburst at some point or the other. Thus, while pausing and breathing, validate your emotions. You may even say this to yourself, 'I am feeling anger right now, it will pass, it is just an emotion.' Remind yourself, 'Everything is okay, my child and I are safe, there is no danger' so that your body starts calming down and your response is more in your control.

The pause can range from ten seconds to ten minutes, depending on the circumstances. As the pause may not come naturally when you start to practise, you may even draw a pause sign with a pen on your wrist or at the back of your hand to remind you in difficult times. It will help you save yourself from the damage of your own behaviour in different situations. Remember, it is just that moment that you need to let pass; once it passes, you will not want to behave in that way at all.

3. What should I do if can't stay calm?

First, know that it is okay. It is good for our children to see us as humans and not as idols of perfection. When we make a mistake, we can treat it as an opportunity for us to model in front of our children, how we can learn from these situations, apologize and take responsibility for our behaviour without being hard on ourselves. We need children to not only learn how to avoid making mistakes but also how to behave after they mess up; after all, it is going to happen. If we think about it, we learn and grow through mistakes much more than when we do something right.

It is important here to remember to be careful to not blame your child in subtle ways for your own behaviour. For example, don't say something like, 'I am sorry, but you were not listening so I had to get angry.' This is not the right kind of apology. Here, instead of taking responsibility for our reaction, we are putting the onus on the child.

We must be genuine when saying sorry and we must take responsibility for our words and actions. Try something like, 'I am sorry I was not feeling good and couldn't control myself.'

Please be kind to yourself even after you mess up. In fact, show more love to yourself because you were going through something difficult emotionally which made you react in an unhelpful way. When we learn to forgive ourselves, we also learn to forgive our children for their mistakes. In learning to be calm parents, we are making a journey towards loving and accepting ourselves and our children in the process. We are investing in a beautiful and real relationship with our children and not an ideal one.

IV

DISCIPLINE

How to discipline children and create boundaries
using calm and connection

11

Why Do We Need Discipline?

'What does it mean to discipline my child?'
'How can I discipline while being calm?'
'How much discipline is too much discipline?'
*'Where should I discipline my child and where can
I let my child be?'*

When we hear the word 'discipline', we picture parents as authoritative figures, who are correcting their children and regulating their behaviour, telling them what to do and what not to do. We also tend to believe that well-disciplined children follow rules and boundaries without questioning them and do not test boundaries. We see discipline in the form of parents scolding children or punishing them for their mistakes, and the children understanding and following what parents are saying.

But this is not the kind of discipline that I am talking about. In this section, I will discuss positive discipline—what we mean by it, how we achieve it with our children and how it is different from the description of discipline in the previous paragraph.

Before diving into 'how to discipline', let us first understand why we need discipline at all with our children and what we aim to achieve by it.

We need discipline to:

- *Keep children safe*
  Children's brains are still developing and thus, they are impulsive, lack emotional regulation and are unable to predict the consequences of their own actions or make rational decisions. Our children's safety is our responsibility and accordingly, we need to put in place some boundaries in the form of discipline to keep our children safe.
  For example, two-year-olds need constant supervision so that they do not hurt themselves or others in their physical environment. Though eight-year-olds understand their physical environment, they are still making sense of how the world works and their perspective is limited, so we are naturally concerned about their emotional needs and ensuring their safety from the outside world, from predators online or offline and so on.
  While keeping our children safe, we also need to give them space to explore and refrain from restricting

them so much that it hampers their healthy growth and development. We have to remind ourselves that we cannot protect our children from every difficult experience and that we also need to give them space to allow them to make their own mistakes and learn from them. It is a tough balance to keep and a hard battle with ourselves to decide where to let go and where to step in to protect them. I hope the following pages will help you find some answers about these.

- *Teach children about appropriate and inappropriate behaviour*

While children are exploring their surroundings, they are also experimenting with different kinds of behaviours and learning which behaviours work and which do not. As discussed earlier, our children's brains are not developed completely at a young age and thus, are not equipped to handle all emotions. We also know that children behave based on what they feel, without any filter. They may often hit or throw things, become rude or use bad words, and may hurt others physically or emotionally without having a complete understanding of the impact of their behaviour.

Therefore, a large part of disciplining children is setting boundaries to limit their inappropriate behaviours and helping them learn to express themselves in better ways. At the same time, we must remember that we cannot expect children to behave perfectly all the time; so we need to be patient and increase our tolerance towards some behaviours, especially the ones that are not harmful and are just aspects of being a child.

- *Help children follow a routine*
We have to accomplish so many tasks with our children every day—getting them to eat, sleep and complete their homework, sending them to school and so on. Having a routine around these tasks and helping children follow it is an essential part of disciplining them. Having a predictable routine helps children feel safe as they know what to expect. However, at times, children resist following the planned routine and do not cooperate. But we can deal with these situations effectively with the concept of positive discipline that we will discuss in the following chapters.

- *Help children learn the right values*
Our children are ultimately going to be a part of society as they are the next generation. As parents, it is expected that we feel responsible for raising them right and instilling the correct values in them. We want them to be kind, successful, compassionate, independent, responsible and so much more. Discipline is a tool that helps in making our children imbibe these values.

But then again, we must keep in mind that children take time to internalize these values and must be realistic about our expectations—they are learning every day, but what they learn takes time to show up in their behaviour as they grow. Parenting is similar to sowing seeds which will bear flowers of wisdom as the plant grows with time—we just need to play our part right.

While children are growing, they experiment with a lot of behaviours through different stages and ages. These behaviours are a part of their journey of learning and do not necessarily become a part of their personality. It is important to keep this in mind so that we don't get too worried about each and every negative behaviour of our children and overreact. How we respond to our children's behaviours at different stages also matters a great deal in shaping their personalities.

As parents, we need to keep the whole picture in mind. Remember, a three-year-old who hits does not lead to the child becoming a thirty-year-old who continues to hit. Children keep changing as their brains develop, becoming more sophisticated and mature with time.

- *Help our children's brains understand the concept of boundaries*
  Children's brains are constantly forming neural connections based on their experiences in the environment around them. In a way, these connections are data for them that they then use to make sense of the world. If we want children to understand that there are certain boundaries that they need to follow by the time they are older, then they need to experience some boundaries when they are little as well. Of course, these boundaries

need to be age-appropriate and have to be put in place with respect.

I say this here because I have sometimes heard parents express the opinion that when children are very young, we should let them do whatever they want and as they grow, they will understand and start behaving. I have heard them say things such as, 'He is just a child, let him hit.' Though a two-year-old hitting others is a common behaviour at their age, it does not mean we do not stop the child at all. Another example is giving children what they want because of their stubborn behaviour, assuming that they will understand with age. Here, what the child understands is that the stubborn behaviour is helpful for them and they should repeat it. We need to enforce positive discipline for their brain to experience some boundaries and form the right connections.

In the next chapter, we will look at some forms of discipline that we are familiar with but often do not work well. We will see why these don't work and, in fact, have a negative impact on our children as well as us.

12

Common Ways of Disciplining Children and Why They Don't Work

The Way We Discipline Matters

There are many ways in which we are already trying to discipline our children and get them to cooperate with us. We explain things to them, get angry at them, threaten them or give them a time-out, try to bribe them into doing something, and some of us also raise our hands to correct them or teach them the right ways.

If we think about it, there are two goals that we want to achieve by disciplining our children.

1. In-the-moment discipline: This is our short-term goal where we need to set boundaries at that moment and need our child to cooperate with us. For example, when we need to go out and ask our child to put on their shoes but they refuse or when

we need to take our child to school and they refuse to get ready for school, or even when our child behaves in an inappropriate way such as by hitting or throwing things and we need to stop them.

2. Long-term discipline: This includes the long-term goals we have for our children. With time, we want that our children should:

   a. start cooperating more with us as they grow so that our struggles are reduced

   b. learn to regulate their emotions better as their brain develops and act more maturely with age

   c. behave better, not only around us but also when we are not around them. We want them to learn to 'self-regulate'

   d. become more responsible and independent in their tasks by following routines on their own without us reminding them to do things all the time; and

   e. grow into kind and compassionate human beings who can form beautiful relationships, be mature and find success in their lives.

The way we discipline our children in any given moment to meet our short-term goal of stopping unwanted behaviour or to make the child listen to us immediately plays a very important role in what will be the long-term effect on our children. It will determine if we are moving towards our ultimate parenting goals or not.

So, let us discuss the techniques we may already be using with our children to solve immediate situations and make them cooperate with us. We will also see what these techniques are doing in the long term for us—are they really helping or are they actually creating long-term troubles?

• **Anger**

Getting angry at our children, and showing that anger through our tone and volume of voice, expressions and gestures is a common practice in parenting. The intensity of anger may vary from situation to situation and from parent to parent but one thing is sure—it does seem to work and it is often the most natural response from parents when facing a challenging situation with their children. After all, while we do not need to think twice before getting angry, being calm takes much more effort.

We have already discussed the effects of parenting by using anger in detail in the 'calm parenting' section of this book. Here, I want to remind you what anger does to the parent–child dynamic in the long term:

✓ As we keep using anger with our children, they get more and more immune to our rage and thus, become more stubborn.
✓ Anger only works till the time the child allows it to work on them and then comes a time when it ultimately backfires.

✓ By observing us, children learn to be angry and start showing similar patterns of behaviour.

✓ Once children get used to our anger, they stop responding to our calm tone and wait for us to get angry before they pay us any heed.

✓ Excessive use of anger takes a toll on our long-term relationship with our children and disconnects us from them.

• **Timeouts**

I have heard many professionals recommending that children should be given timeouts for unacceptable behaviour. This means sending the child to sit in a corner or on a chair for a few minutes to calm down, reflect and learn from their mistakes.

Based on my own experience as a parent and from understanding how the brain reacts to timeouts from the book *No-Drama Discipline* by Daniel Siegel and Tina Payne Bryson, I have realized that the timeout strategy does not work due to the following reasons:[1]

✓ Firstly, our children's brains are not developed enough to self-reflect or self-soothe. They need our help to regulate and learn better behaviours, which we can help them do by connecting with their emotions and setting boundaries calmly, respectfully and firmly. Sending children to a timeout disconnects us from them and they are hardly able to comprehend the situation or derive any lessons from it.

✓ Secondly, if the child refuses to comply with the timeout, then it leads to another fight or argument between the parent and the child. This is what happened when I experimented with the timeout technique with my son when he was three. He would get up from the chair repeatedly, which became a new issue between us, and the actual problem that had led to the timeout in the first place lost all relevance. After all, we need our children's cooperation to make them sit still for the timeout as we cannot force their actions in any way.

✓ Thirdly, the way timeouts are supposed to be implemented is not actually followed by parents. Timeouts are to be put in place respectfully and firmly while being kind and empathetic with our children. But most of the time, parents enforce it with anger, making it sound like a punishment, which completely destroys the whole purpose of a timeout. Instead of the child being able to reflect on their own behaviour, they get more upset and resentful.

• Bribes

We offer bribes or incentives to our children when we really need them to do something or cooperate with us. It may look something like this:

'If you switch off the screen now, I will give you chocolate.'

'If you do your homework right now, I will get you new stickers.'

'If you are well-behaved at the party, I will give you a toy on our way back.'

Bribes seem like the perfect way to go because they do not involve any negative interactions, the child cooperates with the parents and is happy. It is apparently a win-win situation. But when we use bribes repeatedly, this is what happens in the long term:

- ✓ The bribe that we use to get a task done stops working after a point. This means that even if we offer the chocolate or toy as before, the child will not cooperate with us. So, we will have to increase the value of our bribes to get the same things done by our children.

- ✓ Children who get used to bribes start demanding them to do just about anything for us. Instead of becoming self-motivated to do an activity, bribes become their motivation in the long run.

- ✓ And in case you are a parent who promises to give something but does not really mean it (that is, you use a false promise to get a task done), then your child will stop trusting your words. In the long run, your words will lose value and will not be effective in getting your child's cooperation.

- • **Hitting and spanking**

Some parents believe that hitting children teaches them a lesson and makes them behave better with time. So, whenever they are unable to control the child using words, they raise their hands to make the children listen to them. Let us see what happens when we hit children to discipline them:

✓ Hitting children makes them lose confidence:
   When we hit children, they feel insulted and disrespected. Consider this: If we are not respected in our own house, how will we demand respect from other people when we go out? When a child is hit in their own home, it affects their self-esteem, which in turn makes them more prone to getting bullied by other children at school. This happens because they feel that they deserve to be treated badly and that they are not good enough.
   Sometimes, it may seem like hitting the child is teaching them to be obedient. Parents generally say, 'My child is well-mannered because I disciplined him by hitting him.' The truth is, that children start suppressing their emotions when they are hit. They may seem well-mannered from the outside but they struggle from the inside and are usually trying to please everyone. You will see such children displaying low levels of confidence in social settings or being too hard on themselves in the long run. They will not be able to accept their mistakes, develop a pattern of negative self-talk and find it hard to develop self-love and self-acceptance in the future. Hitting children kills their true spirit.

✓ Hitting makes children stubborn
   When we hit children in the name of discipline, they
   become immune to our anger and are hardened
   to become more stubborn. This happens because
   these children feel disrespected, misunderstood
   and helpless. These feelings make them defiant
   and they stop listening to their parents even more.
   Parents and other people may term these children
   'difficult' but the truth is that these children are
   most probably suffering emotionally and thus,
   are getting more and more dysregulated in their
   behaviour. They actually need help in the form
   of connection, empathy, kindness and respectful
   boundaries from adults around them.

✓ Hitting children makes them lie and hide things
   from us
   When parents are unable to regulate their reactions
   towards their children and hit them, children
   automatically start hiding things to protect themselves
   from their parent's reactions. These children will
   begin to lie as they feel their parents cannot handle
   the truth. This creates such a distance between the
   parent and the child that the parent ends up being
   blind towards what is happening in the child's life.
   That's scary because it means that the parents are no
   longer able to protect their children. This is because
   instead of coming to us parents at the time of trouble,
   children will run and hide from us, and may end up
   getting into bigger trouble.

✓ Children who are hit at home may tend to become
   bullies outside:

This happens because the hard fact is that they are being bullied by their own parents at home. This may sound like a very hard pill to swallow, but it is the truth. Children who become bullies are usually the ones who are not getting the love and understanding that they need at home. They are emotionally disconnected from their parents and feel so powerless in their own homes that they try to feel powerful outside by bullying others. They are following the same pattern of behaviour that they are observing in their own family.

However, not all children who are hit become bullies; some may get bullied too (as I mentioned in the first point). What the outcome of being hit by parents will be, depends on the temperament of the child and how it is affecting their unique brain.

✓ Children who are hit develop anxiety at an early age as they feel unsafe:

Children look to their parents for love and protection. When these same parents end up hitting or hurting them, children get confused and doubt their own safety. They love their parents but still feel unsafe around them, and this triggers anxiety in them at an early age. The neural connections in their brains are formed in such a way that when these children become parents themselves, they find it hard to regulate their behaviour around their own children. They often end up following the same pattern and hitting their kids in the same way, unless and until they consciously change and heal themselves to break the cycle.

✓ Hitting does not work in the long term

If in case you are a parent who is hitting your child to discipline him or her and get them to cooperate, you need to know that the effectiveness of this technique has an expiry date. That means a time will come when you will see that even using physical violence is not helping you in getting your child to cooperate. As I mentioned earlier, children do get more stubborn with age. This may happen at any age according to the temperament of the child. In my experience, children who are strong-willed will rebel earlier, perhaps even at the age of five or six. Some children might wait till they are in their teens to rebel. But hitting children will backfire at some point as they grow up.

I hope this chapter has given you the whole perspective on the techniques we use to discipline children that do not help us in the long term. Sometimes, we are so anxious in order to get our children to cooperate with us at a particular moment that we forget the impact of our behaviour in the long term. In the next chapter, I will discuss what positive discipline entails and how it helps us reach our long-term parenting goals better for our children. Not only that, but it also keeps our children's true spirit intact and helps us create a beautiful relationship with them in spite of having rules and boundaries in place.

13

Positive Discipline and Why We Should Choose It

Now let us talk about what it means to have positive discipline and how we can put it in place in our lives. In this chapter, I will discuss four main aspects of positive discipline that will help to make the concept clearer and explain what positive discipline is and what it is essentially not.

Let us begin by understanding how positive discipline works in our day-to-day lives and how it helps us in reaching our long-term goals better. We will learn where and how to set boundaries for our children and the way to reinforce them without getting angry with our kids. I will delineate the basic concepts of positive discipline in detail using examples and real-life experiences so that you can develop a clear picture of what positive discipline at home looks like.

1. We do not discipline each and every behaviour of the child

If we want our discipline to be effective, we need to make it **realistic** and **achievable** for the child. What we mean by this is that we must remember that children are going to behave like children and thus, we need to have realistic expectations from them according to their age, temperament and capability. Correcting every behaviour of the child that might seem inappropriate to us and asking them to behave in ways that they are not developmentally capable of, are counterproductive. This makes them irritable and possibly more defiant.

Here's an example:

When I took my five-year-old son Saiveer to a restaurant, he kept moving here and there, touching the plate, getting paper napkins from another table—that is, he was generally restless. His father kept telling him, 'Sit properly, why can't you sit in one place, stop moving so much.'

The fact is that it was very difficult for Saiveer to sit in one place and wait for the food while doing nothing. Young children cannot sit idle for too long and keep moving constantly as it is a developmental characteristic. With age, their attention span and capacity to sit increases.

Expecting Saiveer to sit without moving in the restaurant was completely unrealistic and so, he was unable to follow his father's instructions. Instead, because of the constant chiding, he was getting more wayward. He even poured ketchup into a glass of water on the table just because he had nothing else to do.

I had to intervene here and say, 'I can see you are unable to sit without doing anything. Let us ask for a pen and paper from the reception and draw something.' Thankfully, we got the pen and paper, and this gave us ten minutes of him being busy with it, by which time our food was served.

For the rest of the time in the restaurant as well, I had to allow him to get up and move, under the condition that he was not going to damage or spoil anything. Being realistic about my expectations of him helped my son cooperate with my instructions.

Some parents may say here, 'But there are other five-year-olds who are perfectly capable of sitting properly; only my child was behaving restlessly like that.' Well, this is because all children are different, and it is important that we understand our child's unique personality. Some children have more energy than others (as in the case of my son), some may display greater social skills than others, some may write clear letter formations because of their fine motor skills and some may be good at public speaking—the list is endless. When we accept our children for who they are and understand their unique qualities and strengths while making peace with their weaknesses; when we discipline in a way that is achievable for the child and do not expect perfection from them; when we remember to connect with them even while putting in place boundaries, they start cooperating more with us and disciplining them becomes much easier and more manageable.

It is also important to note that **discipline becomes ineffective when we overdo it.** As we have seen, this happens when we correct each and every behaviour of our child. It makes the child immune to our words and they stop responding to us—when it is really important for us that they listen, they do not pay heed to us.

For example:

There are two siblings (five and seven years old) playing together. Their father has a tendency to keep instructing and correcting their behaviour. He says things like:

'Don't talk like that to your sister.'

'Don't be so loud, why are you shouting like that?'

'Be careful, don't dirty anything.'

When two children are playing, it is only natural that they will be loud and will talk in different ways with each other. If we rebuke each and every thing the children do, they will simply tune out and not listen to us when we really need them to.

Here's a scenario:

Say the two siblings are about to hit each other or are about to jump from a place that is unsafe. At such a time, we need them to stop immediately. But our instruction of stopping the harmful behaviour may get lost due to the excessive unimportant instructions that we may have given them when we were correcting them too much. *When we choose where to correct and don't bother too much about behaviours that are age-appropriate and unharmful, we can increase the value of our words in other situations.*

So, while putting discipline in place, we need to remember that children cannot behave according to our expectations all the time and need space to be themselves. Also, children have a natural curiosity to explore and test things. For instance, a one-year-old throws things to experiment with the concept of gravity and how things fall instead of flying in the air. We do obviously have to stop them from breaking and damaging things by removing them from their reach, but we certainly should not overreact and get too impatient with them.

Letting children explore new things under safe boundaries helps their brains develop. For instance, my six-year-old would want to mix different ingredients from the kitchen to see how the mixtures turn out and touch them to feel their textures. From an adult's perspective, he was making a mess; but for him, it was an opportunity to experiment with different textures, indulge in sensory play and learn about cause and effect. So, as his parent, instead of stopping him, I would give him broad boundaries like 'don't do it on the bed' and 'don't waste too much and use only the ingredients that I provide in the tray'. This would give him space to be creative and fulfil his curiosity, but at the same time, he would learn to follow boundaries.

I will talk about how well-laid consequences help in such situations as well in the next chapter.

But, here, my aim is to help you understand how we can still have discipline while giving children opportunities to be themselves and explore, and learn in safe spaces without restricting them too much or correcting every behaviour.

2. We are calm and firm and not angry and impatient while putting boundaries in place

We assume that calm parents do not discipline their children enough and let them do what they want. Parents often express this concern: 'If I do not shout at my child or get angry, people around me judge me for not teaching my child the right behaviour.'

Being calm does not mean that we are not teaching our children the right behaviours or not reinforcing the boundaries correctly. In fact, what we are doing is being kind and compassionate even while disciplining our children. We have discussed this in the previous section of the book as well—being calm does not mean being lenient. Here, I want to elaborate on what ways discipline indeed becomes more effective when we are calm and respectful:

- When we are calm, we look like the authority who is in control

Being calm in our body, tone and behaviour shows that we are in control of ourselves and our emotions. We are the authority figures for our children—giving them permission to do things, forming their routines, and telling them what to do and what not to do. Only when we are in control of ourselves will we be able to look like an effective authority figure.

Imagine a parent shouting in an irritated tone at their child and saying, 'Why are you not listening to me? I have told you so many times not to hit, I am so tired of this behaviour!' To someone observing the situation objectively, what does this parent look like? Are they in control or out of control? When a parent behaves like this, chances are that the child will get even more dysregulated. As a result, instead of the child's undesirable behaviour stopping, problems might increase.

When we follow positive discipline, we practise using a tone that is firm and not angry. When we are firm, this is what we look like: our body is calm, we use fewer words, our tone is in control and our message is to the point. A firm tone is not affected by emotion as we do not let ourselves get intimidated by the behaviour of our children; instead, we pause, breathe and regulate ourselves, if required. We may also add the element of empathy while being firm. For example, you can consider saying things like the following when firmly setting boundaries:

✓ *'We have to complete our work now. I can see you are having a hard time with the sheet. Let me help you, but we are going to finish it before we go to play. I know you can do it.'*

✓ *'We cannot use our hands like this. I will have to pick you up to help you not hurt your friend. I think you got really angry, but we still need to control our hands.'*

✓ *'I can see you really wanted to play with water, but the weather is cold and we will not play with it right now.'*

Sometimes, we need to pause after instructing the child and allow them to process the instruction and respond to it instead of repeating the instruction over and over again. Children respond better when we say less and observe more, giving them time to follow the instructions. Thus, we must be patient and respectful while keeping the boundary intact.

• When we are calm, our children can regulate better and choose better behaviours.

When we are regulated in our body from the inside and in our behaviour from the outside, the chances of our children cooperating with us increase tremendously. It may sound difficult to believe but it is true—only when you experiment with this and see the results for yourself, will you be able to see how effective it is. And remember, being calm inside matters a lot more than only looking calm from the outside. I will give you my own example here:

Let us suppose that my six-year-old son Saiveer is watching something on the iPad and it is time for him to turn it off. But he does not want to do it. Here, I can enforce the boundary by either being calm or losing control. Let's see how these two scenarios can play out.

Situation 1: Saiveer tells me he doesn't want to switch off the iPad and I get angry and say, 'You HAVE to stop. You promised you would give back the tablet after this video ends.' But he does not budge. So in order to follow the boundary I have previously set, I try to snatch the screen away from him. Here, my son pulls the screen back and now we are physically fighting for the screen, pulling it from two ends. Even if I am successful in getting his grip off the iPad, I will then have to deal with his meltdown, where he will become dysregulated. He may start crying, arguing, shouting or even say, 'I will break your phone too', just because he is feeling powerless.

Situation 2: Saiveer tells me he doesn't want to switch off the iPad. I respond in a kind tone and say, 'I can see you don't'. I go to my son and then firmly say, 'But we still have to beta.* *Here, he says, 'But I don't want to and I will not.' I first try connecting with him with the reply, 'Hmm, you love this show, right? This character is really funny. But you can watch it later. If you don't switch it off, I will have to do it for you [putting the boundary firmly].'*

---

* Son.

I wait for fifteen to twenty seconds and then say, 'Do you need me to do it?' and put my hand on the device in a gesture of taking it. I pull it half an inch, giving him a chance to turn off the device himself. Here, I want to point out that my hand is gentle but firm and I am giving him the opportunity to cooperate on his own. I also add a line to encourage him to cooperate, 'I know you can stop even if it is hard', giving him another ten seconds.

Here, in most cases, he lets the screen go in a couple of minutes, though unwillingly. In case he tries to pull the screen back, I do not pull away the screen forcefully. Instead, I keep my hand on the iPad and say, 'You will switch it off now and we are going to play something else or I will have to do it for you.' If we maintain our calm till this point, the child will let go of the screen. In case there is a tantrum after this, we deal with it with empathy and by letting it pass without giving in or losing our calm.

In case you are a parent reading this and thinking, 'My child would not give the screen even in this situation', then read on.

- Hug your child, switch off the screen gently but firmly, and deal with the tantrum that may follow. Or you might put a consequence here (like the next iPad time may be sacrificed), which is a tactic that I will discuss in the next section. But, under no circumstance will we indulge in a physical fight with our child to get hold of the device.

- Consider delving deeper to understand the reason behind your child's stubborn behaviour and check if there is a disconnection that needs to be dealt with first. Are there inconsistent boundaries because of which the child is testing you more? Or perhaps the child is feeling powerless or misunderstood during other parts of the day? If you experience more episodes of negative behavior from the child, it is time to look at the broader picture that might be increasing your everyday struggles with your children.

Remember, it is easier to be calm when our children are listening to us. It is when they are not listening that we need to make sure that we regulate our emotions and body and still be calm because that will be our real victory. As we have seen before, we can only control our own behaviour; how our children will react in the moment is beyond our control. But when we consciously work on keeping our body and behaviour calm and firm, our children's behaviour gets much less dysregulated than when we lose control over our emotions and behaviour.

I completely understand how difficult it may get sometimes to remain calm in some situations. But by practising taking a pause (which we talked about in the section 'Calm') and by breathing consciously in the moment of crisis while keeping our thoughts in check (as thoughts lead to feelings and behaviour as discussed in the earlier chapter), we can keep our calm in most circumstances. We also need to remember to keep our expectations from our children and situations realistic and not take our children's behaviour personally.

We are calmer as parents when we have realistic expectations from our kids.

In the example I gave of my son with the iPad, if I expect my son to never show resistance while switching off the screen, I will get extremely angry every time he does not listen to me. But I have to remember that screens are very addictive, and it is difficult for my child to stop and he may need my help.

Also, in the example of the restaurant I gave earlier when my son kept moving around restlessly, my husband got irritated whereas I was able to be patient. This was because I was not really expecting my son to sit in one place without doing anything. This is when I told my husband, 'You know he can't just sit and do nothing at his age. Even we cannot sit like that and will soon start scrolling through our phones. So let's be realistic.' This made my husband considerably calmer at that moment.

Effectively disciplining our children does not mean they will never say no to us or try to test the boundaries put in place. It is how we respond in those situations that will have the most impact and make the discipline positive. When we try to focus on what reasons could cause our children to behave in certain ways, instead of getting fixated on why our children are being so unreasonable, it becomes easier for us parents to be calmer and thus, have effective boundaries with our children.

3. We use the connection to gain cooperation

In Section II ('Connection'), I talked about how building a connection helps us in increasing our influence over our children's behaviour and gaining their cooperation. If our children do not cooperate with us, is it even possible to discipline them? We do try to make our children listen to us in many ways—by showing anger, giving bribes, issuing threats or even hitting them—and we have seen how these techniques actually don't work and create more problems for us in the long term. When incorporating positive discipline in our parenting, we must invest in building connections with children so that they listen to us more. When we are successful in building a connection, half the battle is won.

There are two ways in which we use the connection:

1. We build connections during an ongoing challenging situation

    In a situation where our child is not cooperating with us or not respecting the boundary we have set, we have to try to form a connection at that moment to help them cooperate better. We do this in the following way:

•   We stay calm and regulated:
    We keep our calm to maintain our connection in the situation. Whenever we get dysregulated (angry, upset or anxious) while disciplining our children, we lose our connection and our message stops getting across to them, their brains being unable to

process what is happening. This is another reason our children tend to cooperate more when we are calm and firm instead of when we are angry or irritated in a crisis.

- We try to be playful instead of getting irritated: Sometimes, just keeping our patience and being more playful with our kids helps prevent a bad situation from getting worse. Whenever I tell parents to be more patient, they say, 'I do try to keep patience, but my child still does not listen.' I wonder if that parent understands what it means to show patience.

Let me give you an example of a situation to clarify what I mean by being patient and playful:

It is morning and Saiveer is getting ready for school. Being a six-year-old, he needs constant reminders to hurry up and is unable to follow the morning routine to get ready on his own. At the last moment, when it is time to leave home for school, my son hides behind his play tent. I can respond in two ways in this instance.

Without being playful: 'Saiveer, we are getting late, why are you doing this? Come out now.'

With patience and being playful: 'Oh, where is my Saiveer? Is he behind the tent? I found you!'

I have tried responding in both these ways. When I adopt the latter response, my child comes out laughing and continues towards the door with me. But when I lose patience and instruct him to not hide and hurry up, it makes the situation negative, my son gets irritable and I end up shouting at him while sending him to school.

We can always choose how we want to respond to a behaviour, but we can only make that choice consciously when we are aware and mindful. Here, parents may say, 'But there is no time to be playful when we are getting late.' My answer to them is that both responses, the irritated one and the playful one, take the same amount of time. We do not have to go out of our way to be patient and playful as it takes the same five seconds as responding in any other way. In fact, the child reacts better when we are playful and it ultimately saves us time. Another example may be that while my child is practising his handwriting, I make playful comments like, 'The "t" just got hurt on his bum' or 'The "f" is upset because his head got hurt' instead of just saying 'Write properly'. These comments make him laugh and feel less irritated than when I correct him in a serious tone. Changing the tone of my comments also helps me maintain his interest in writing.

When we apply this technique in everyday situations, the situations become less stressful for us and our children.

- We validate and empathize:
  Whenever we put a boundary in place, our children may express that they are not happy with it. For instance, when we tell them to do homework, they may say, '*I don't want to*'; when we tell them to

stop playing and get ready for the class, they may say, '*No, I want to play more.*' First, we must remember that children are just expressing what they are feeling and their words do not indicate if they will actually do what we are asking or not. When we understand this simple difference, then instead of reacting, we can respond to their behaviour with more empathy.

It is our responsibility as parents to get our children to do their homework or send them to school. But we can validate their feelings instead of repeatedly instructing them or arguing with them because of their reactions. When we validate what they are feeling, we can form an instant connection.

For instance, we can say: '*I know you don't want to stop and I can see you are enjoying this, but we can only give this one more minute and then we have to stop. I know you can do it.*'

Also, instead of saying this from a distance, it is better to be physically close to our children when instructing or speaking to them. If we can, we should go to the child and make contact by gently placing a hand on the shoulder or even making eye contact.

- We explain less and ask more:
  To build a connection in a particular moment, it is better to avoid a common mistake that parents make, i.e. providing long or repeated explanations on why the task at hand is important to do.

Instead, it is better to involve the children in two-way communication by posing more questions to them, which helps them to process a situation and respond accordingly. This ensures that our children are listening to us and that our message is getting across to them. It is also important to incorporate pauses in the conversation. Sometimes our children take some time to respond, and when we pause for ten to fifteen seconds, we realize that they do cooperate—it may just take a few seconds instead of being instantaneous. At times, when I control myself from getting irritated with my son and wait for a few seconds for him to respond, I find that my child decides within that time to cooperate. Then I am actually relieved that I controlled my initial reaction of irritation because then the situation would have taken a more negative direction.

For example, observe this conversation between a parent and a child.

Child: I don't want to do the homework.
Parent: I can see that you find it boring sometimes, don't you?
Child: Yes I do; I will not do it.
Parent: Hmm, and when ma'am asks you to submit the homework tomorrow, what will you do?
Here, we allow the child to take a minute to process this. After the pause, the conversation can go on.

Parent: I know you will do it and submit it. Do you need my help here or do you want to do it on your own? (Giving the child options.)

Child: No, it's boring.

Parent: I know, that's why we will do it superfast and finish quickly. Then we'll have free time.

Child: I don't want to.

Here, the parent does not respond to the last comment and pauses for a couple of minutes because the child is simply repeating the conversation and the parent does not want to indulge in arguments or repeated explanations.

Parent, after the pause: We have to complete our work. Let's finish it fast so that we can go out.

Even if the child is whining at this point, the parent is calm and firm and helps the child in completing the homework with patience.

If you observe the conversation, you'll notice a few things:

✓ The parent is posing questions instead of explaining, such as saying things like, 'Homework is important, you have to take it to school tomorrow', which is a common way parents respond in these situations.

✓ The parent includes empathy while instructing the child.

✓ The parent does not get irritated and avoids using words like 'Why do you always behave like this?'

or 'You are such a bad child for not doing your homework.'

✓ The parent's tone is not angry but firm. Instead of requesting the child to do the task, the parent is laying down the boundary, being authoritative and respectful at the same time.

✓ The parent is also trying to give options to the child, asking if they want help or want to do the task on their own. Here, parents can also give options like, 'Do you want to do it on the bed or on the study table?' Providing options gives the child some control over a situation.

✓ I want to highlight that even in the last sentence of the conversation, the parent is not offering a bribe but helping the child see what comes after the work. This helps the child feel better in that moment and helps them cooperate.

(If the child still does not do the homework, then it is important to probe the underlying reason that is causing the behaviour. In the next section, I talk about the consequences that we may need to use if the child repeatedly refuses to cooperate with us.)

When we follow these points, we successfully form a connection that helps in disciplining children without us getting angry. When using positive discipline in this way, the everyday process of doing a task like homework becomes easier as there is less negativity attached to it.

Remember, disconnection occurs when:

✓ We get irritated and anxious;
✓ We start giving explanations and arguing with the child; and
✓ We threaten them and forget to empathize with what they are feeling.

2. We build connections in our daily interactions with our children

In Chapter 5, we talked about giving respect to our children, not correcting them all the time, being more positive with them, and listening to them and empathizing with them in our day-to-day communication to build a better long-term connection with them.

The crux here is that when children generally feel good about the relationship that they share with us, we face fewer challenges with them when it comes to helping them follow boundaries.

Here's an example: I have to take my child to a birthday party in the evening. In the first half of the same day, I keep losing my patience with my child because of my work pressure. Even before leaving the house, we get into an argument about the clothes he wants to wear. By the time we sit in the car, my child and I have had lots of negative interactions during the day.

At the birthday party, my child does not seem to listen to me or cooperate with me when I need his cooperation. I try to empathize and form a connection by physically coming down to my child's level and making eye contact. I try to be calm and firm but nothing seems to work. Here, I may blame the child for being completely unreasonable but the fact is that the child is already feeling disconnected due to our negative interactions throughout the day and this has reduced my influence over my child.

It is not only how we deal with the child in the moment of a challenging situation that is important, but it is also the quality of the overall relationship with the child that matters. When parents tell me, 'My child gives me a hard time during studies or when the guests are over', my question to them is, how is your interaction with your child during other times of the day?

Building a connection with children is not manipulating them into cooperating with us—it is bettering the quality of our relationship with our children, allowing us to have a genuine human relationship with them where there is more love, understanding and acceptance. When we invest in the overall connection with our kids, we get their willing cooperation at most times and thus, discipline becomes comparatively easier. Do read through Section II in case you need some tips on how we can build this connection.

4. **Positive discipline means having firm and respectful boundaries**

As I have mentioned before, children need boundaries. When we fail to guide our children with consistent and predictable boundaries, it affects their behaviour as they do not know where to stop. A common misconception that goes with gentle parenting is that gentle parents do not say no to their children and when they do say no, their children always listen to them because they are being gentle. But this is not the case.

Firstly, even when we are being gentle and calm as parents, we are responsible for setting boundaries for our children. I will share an experience of a client here to give more perspective on what I mean:

Mausami* wanted to change her parenting style for her four-year-old child Milli. She had been unconsciously following a parenting style that was similar to the way she had been parented—she was used to yelling a lot and raising her hand at her daughter to discipline her. She was struggling because Milli was a strong-willed girl who was responding to her mother with the same behaviours that she was being subjected to—she was rebelling with the same tone, gestures and a lot of uncontrolled anger. In the first couple of sessions with Mausami, I helped her understand connection and how it works. To my surprise, Mausami completely transformed her parenting approach and was very happy with the changes in her child and her relationship with her.

But after a month, Mausami called me crying and said, 'I completely lost it with my daughter after a month of working on being gentle. I yelled and hit her

---

* Name changed.

and I feel so lost and overwhelmed.' She then explained to me that her daughter had been bossing Mausami around too much and had stopped listening to her. Upon further discussion with Mausami, I realized that she was giving her four-year-old child too much power, which her daughter was unable to handle. Mausami was not being firm when required and was allowing her daughter to do what she wanted at all times, even when it was unreasonable. For example, if Milli hit her mom, Mausami would tolerate it. Mausami would let Milli throw things around, and then leave the room if her daughter asked her to leave. Mausami, as the adult, was not setting the boundaries which Milli desperately needed and was asking for, by testing her mother more and more. (Also the change in Mausami's parenting style was so drastic and sudden that her daughter may have been confused, leading to her testing Mausami's patience even more.)

Mausami got in touch with me at the point where she got very triggered when one day her daughter said to her, 'Have you seen my hand? I am going to slap you so hard.' Mausami completely lost it with Milli and started to yell and hit her. Even later, she regretted the whole episode, she could not understand what was happening.

Mausami had missed the key step of maintaining her boundaries while being calm. Children need boundaries as it makes them feel safe and in control, and actually helps them to behave better. In the absence of boundaries, children do not even understand which behaviour is acceptable and which is not. I recall Mausami saying, '*I remembered to be calm but forgot the word "firm", Dr Ishinna.*' When we are unable to communicate and set clear and consistent boundaries for our children, they end up throwing more tantrums and becoming more dysregulated as their brains do not understand where to stop.

5. We must be consistent and predictable with the boundaries we set

While setting boundaries for our children, it is important that we follow through with what we say. When we are consistent with the boundaries we set and maintain, our children know what to expect and they test us less. So, keep the following points in mind:

- **Do not give in to tantrums:** A significant cause of confusion about boundaries in children's minds is when we give in to their tantrums. These are instances when we change our initial 'no' to a 'yes' because of the child crying, shouting, arguing, throwing a fit, etc. When we waver in our decision, children get two messages: first, '*My parent's "no" can be changed, I just need to try harder*'; and second, '*These tantrums help me to get what I want and work in my favour.*' Thus, it is not a child's fault if they are repeating tantrums more often and with increased intensity and duration as they grow.

My clients sometimes tell me, '*If I do not give my child what he wants, he can cry for up to two hours at a stretch.*' I believe them when they say that because their child is trying every possible trick to get their demand fulfilled. The child's past experience has taught him that crying may work sometimes, and thus, they try it every time. It is at this time that I ask the parent, '*Did your child always cry for two hours at a stretch?*' They most often say 'no' and that the duration of crying has increased with time, and has now become unmanageable. Can you see the pattern here?

When we stick to our decisions in spite of our children's crying or any tantrums they throw, they learn that these behaviours do not work for them. And here, I want to remind you that we do not need to get angry to stick to our word. We just need to be calm and empathetic while letting the feeling in the child which is causing the tantrum pass (do take a look at Section I to revise how to handle tantrums).

If we want our children to learn to behave better, we need to stop rewarding the behaviours we do not want them to repeat; instead, we need to reward better behaviours. Also, it is better to say 'yes' to our children when they ask nicely in the first place instead of changing our decision from 'no' to 'yes' later because of a tantrum. To follow this approach, it is important that we pause for a moment and think if we can follow through with our decision before saying 'yes' or 'no' to our children.

When we consistently follow through with our decisions, children stop testing us as much and trust our word when we say it. Here, I always suggest to parents that in case they feel that they will not be able to follow through and stick to a decision—that they may have to ultimately give the child what he or she wants due to the child's behaviour that may follow—then it is always better to say 'yes' in the first place. For example, your eight-year-old tells you he wants to eat a burger and you say no. Here, if your child argues with you for an hour and you ultimately give in and say, 'Fine, but only this time', your child learns that arguments work and they are going to argue more and more in the future to change your decisions.

- **Never use empty threats:** Our children stop trusting our words when we use empty threats with them and do not mean what we say. For example, telling our children, 'I will not give you the ice cream if you do not do your homework' becomes an empty threat if we end up giving them the treat due to a tantrum they throw later in spite of not doing the homework.

    I understand that we sometimes use empty threats so that our children cooperate at that moment and we can solve the current situation. For example, we might need the child to wear a jacket before going out to a birthday party and we may say, 'If you don't wear this jacket right now, I will not take you to the party' just so that our child agrees to wear it, while knowing that leaving the child behind is not an option even if he does not cooperate. Here, if we end up taking the child to the party even when he refuses to put on the jacket, our words simply lose value.

Another common instance of parents not sticking to their word is when children refuse to get in the car or refuse to budge from a place and parents say, 'I am going then, you stay here'. This is obviously something we cannot do and our children stop responding to this threat completely after the first couple of instances. Empty threats take away the credibility of our words and using them confuses children about boundaries. Instead of this empty threat, I suggest we say, '*We have to leave now and you need to sit in the car. If you don't do it on your own, I will have to pick you up and place you in the car because I do not have any other option.*' This is what you will actually do ultimately for a young child. Of course, if your child is at an age where you can't pick them up, then you will not use this sentence. The point is that you must say what you will and can actually do.

When we mean what we say and refrain from using empty threats in our day-to-day lives, our children stop testing our words and boundaries as much. Following this rule has helped me a lot with my son; he now takes my words more seriously than he does of other family members, including his father.

In the next section, we will learn about using consequences—which is different from threats or punishment—with children when we need their cooperation. Consequences are a tool to help children choose to behave better and become more responsible for their actions in the long run.

- **Follow a routine:** Another way of maintaining consistency in our boundaries is by having in place a predictable routine for our children. Routines also make them feel safe as they indicate to them what to expect and their brains are more prepared for what is to come. Children's cooperation also increases when they know what is coming their way instead of when they are randomly instructed to follow orders. Here's an example to illustrate the benefits of a routine.

  I was struggling to do some worksheets which my son's school was sending during the Covid-19 lockdown. As there was no routine in place during the lockdown, I would tell him at different times of the day, 'Let's do the worksheet now', and he would reply with 'Not now.' I would ask again later in the day and his reply would be the same. This became a pattern and I started getting frustrated, asking him multiple times throughout the whole day to complete a ten-minute task.

  So, I built a routine around this work. While preparing his bath, I would also prepare and keep the worksheets on the table for him to do right after getting out of the bath. The minute he was out of the washroom, I would make him do the worksheets and only then would we leave the room. This made it so much easier to work with my son because, with time, he got used to the routine. He even started to sit at his table on his own without prompting after his bath to do his worksheet.

His mind was so prepared to do the worksheets after the bath that sometimes, during the bath, he would ask me, 'Do I need to do the worksheet?' and at times even say, 'I don't want to do it.' In the latter case, I would simply empathize and not argue, but then help him complete his work. The point is that the routine I set up helped his mind be more prepared for what was to come and my struggle was reduced considerably.

I want to emphasize here that even when we build a routine, there will be days when our child may show some resistance to following it. Here, we need to do the following:

a. Be calm and patient and remember that children may also have some off days where they may not be feeling too good. So, be more tolerant on such days because if we get too angry or irritated in reinforcing the routine, it will increase our struggles around the same task in the following days.

b. Reflect on the routine that suits us and our children and whether we have over-scheduled the day. Remember, a routine is supposed to help us, not make us more stressed. If the routine is becoming stressful to follow, edit it and make it easier.

There will also be times when we lay off the routine because of travel, holidays, sickness or family occasions. Whenever we come back to following a routine after a break, we will have to be patient for the first few days in order for the child's brain to readjust to getting back to the normal routine.

When we can keep in mind the information discussed in this chapter while disciplining our children, we will be able to reach our long-term parenting goals better. One thing that we always have to remind ourselves of is that we cannot really control our children's decisions and behaviours. When we try to control them by using anger, threats or punishments, it only solves the immediate situation but ultimately they lead us nowhere, creating more problems for us in the future.

Practising being calm and firm, and making use of connections to influence our children's behaviour while keeping discipline realistic and consistent, takes us a long way as parents. Remember to be kind and respectful even while disciplining children and reinforcing boundaries around them—we do not need to disrespect our kids to discipline them. These principles help us raise individuals who are able to form healthy relationships, become more emotionally mature and resilient, and are able to regulate their behaviour while understanding the concept of healthy boundaries.

In the next chapter, I will answer the question, 'What if the child still does not cooperate in a particular situation?' In such instances, we sometimes have to use consequences, which are not threats or punishments. In fact, they help children become more responsible for their behaviour in the long run. So, keep reading to complete the last piece of the puzzle of positive discipline.

V

CONSEQUENCES

14

What Are Consequences?

A consequence is a result or reaction that is caused because of an action or a situation. As individuals, whenever we decide to engage in a specific behaviour, we have to face the result that follows. We all face the consequences of our actions in our day-to-day lives. For example:

When we run a red light, we may have to pay a fine.

When we drive in a reckless way, we may get into an accident.

When we stay up too late watching TV, we may get a headache in the morning and be tired at work.

Consequences can, of course, be positive or negative. But in this chapter, I will be referring to the ones that may be unpleasant to face or cause us discomfort. As in the above examples, paying a fine may feel embarrassing, the accident can cause us physical pain and cost a lot of money, and the headache may make us less efficient throughout the day.

The common thing that runs through all such experiences is that they are opportunities for learning. Faced with these situations, we learn in two ways:

- Once we have faced a negative consequence arising out of a situation, we understand that we will have to bear the results of our actions. This, hopefully, makes us behave in a more responsible manner subsequently. Because of the negative effects that we had to endure, we will think twice before indulging in such behaviours the next time. So, we might be more cautious while driving because we know things can go wrong otherwise or we might choose to sleep on time to avoid another headache the next day.

  Dealing with the consequences of our actions makes us more mature and enables us to make better decisions. As we are better able to understand the relationship between our behaviours and their effects, we become more far-sighted. This may be one of the reasons why, as we grow older, we move toward healthier choices—we have learnt our lessons from a variety of consequences that we have experienced over time.

- Learning about cause and effect by facing consequences helps in skill building. When we become aware of the results that are likely to happen because of our actions, we have an opportunity to hone our skills based on that learning. Let us consider the example of picking up the skill to drive a car. While learning and training to drive, we make many errors and experience their consequences. If we brake suddenly and feel the car jerk unpleasantly, it teaches us how to apply the brake smoothly the next time. When we make a mistake in estimating the distance between us and the car in front of us and bumping into it, we learn to judge the gaps between vehicles better in the future. All these negative experiences make us more cautious and help us make better decisions, which in turn contribute to us becoming skilled drivers.

Children and Consequences

Just like us, our children are also learning through their experiences every day. They, too, face the consequences of their behaviours—their brains learn with time which behaviours work in their favour and which don't, and they become more responsible as they grow. Of course, how much the child learns depends on what kind of experiences they go through and how their unique personalities respond to those experiences. But one thing is definite: our children learn much more through their first-hand experiences than from us informing and explaining to them how things work.

Let us understand this by looking at the following examples:

- When a child jumps on the sofa, the parent may tell the child many times: '*Do not jump, you may fall and get hurt.*' But it is only when the child actually falls and gets hurt that they learn to be more careful. The child may still end up jumping on the sofa even after experiencing a fall, but this time they know better how to avoid getting hurt. Some children may learn quickly and for others, it may take a couple of falls before they learn—this also depends on the child's age and personality. But surely, experiencing a fall teaches them much more than us telling them that falling may hurt.

- I remember warning my three-year-old about being careful with glasses that could break easily. But most young children, like my son, have not witnessed a glass breaking. So when they hear our warnings about it, those are just words without any meaning; only when they actually see a glass breaking can they associate meaning with what we are telling them about being careful. When my son did ultimately break a glass and got a cut on his hand from that, he became extremely cautious around glasses without me needing to warn him repeatedly. He would even ask for a plastic cup himself to avoid accidentally getting hurt.

- We parents often warn our children to be careful around hot liquids as they may get burnt. One of the most difficult situations I have faced as a parent was when Saiveer was three-and-a-half-years old and got a severe burn on his chest when piping hot tea spilled on him. You can imagine how difficult it must have been to endure the predicament as a parent. But after Saiveer healed, he became extremely cautious around tea. In fact, I didn't need to worry about him being around hot things anymore. I only had to inform him, 'There is hot tea there', and that would make him alert and careful, which was not the case before.

Here, I am certainly not urging parents to let children be hurt severely in order to learn through consequences. The above examples are just to clarify that facing consequences makes children more responsible for their actions in general. As parents, it is our job to protect our children and keep them safe, but sometimes, we overdo it by not allowing them to face the consequences of their actions at all.

Overprotecting children and saving them all the time from experiencing the consequences of their actions also means not allowing them to have learning experiences. As parents, we often expect children to become responsible by just paying heed to the explanations or lectures we give them. Or we expect that they will learn to not do something if we get angry at them. I can completely understand that parents do not want their children to go through uncomfortable or painful situations that arise from negative consequences. While we know our children will have to face the difficult emotions of frustration, anger, disappointment, helplessness and so on, it is very difficult to watch our children go through them. We feel guilty and upset, maybe because we believe that as parents, we always need to protect our children, and that it is our job to keep them happy and never let them go through hardships. But is that really possible? Or is it even the right approach? When parents think like this, they are overestimating and overplaying their roles as parents, which is not good for their children's growth.

What happens when children don't face the consequences of their actions?

When children do not face the repercussions of their behaviours, they do not become responsible individuals.

Let us understand this with an example regarding a child's school homework:

We often find that when a child is not interested in completing their homework and taking it to school, the parents take all the responsibility of making the child complete the work. With every passing day, completing any homework becomes a battle because the parent has to get angry, threaten the child or even hit them to get the task completed. In such a situation, a parent may complain about how the child is not responsible enough to do their work themselves, may stay up late at night to make the child complete the work or may even do the work for the child. But what the parent is unable to do is let the child go to school without doing the homework and face the natural consequence at school of not showing their work to the teacher. If a parent keeps doing this, instead of the child taking an interest in their studies and working earnestly to learn, they end up feeling like the schoolwork is not their responsibility but their parents.

We must understand that for our children to become mature and more responsible for their behaviours, they need to experience some consequences in their lives. When we let children learn from their own experiences, their brains form valuable connections regarding cause and effect, and they are able to choose better behaviours in the future:

'When I do not do my homework, the teacher may get angry.'

'When I jump on the sofa, I may fall down and perhaps even get hurt.'

'When I do not prepare for the exam well, I get lower marks.'

'When I am rude to my friends, they may not play with me.'

'When I use a bad word, people may get angry with me.'

There are so many lessons our children are learning every day. But they cannot learn them without making mistakes and facing their implications. With every experience, our children's brains become a little more mature. It is we parents who have to become more resilient for our children, which may not be easy but is necessary.

Some parents try to protect their children all the time and do not allow them to experience consequences. For example:

They may never let their child fall or get hurt by constantly being around them.

They try to never let their child feel the disappointment of failing an exam by making sure the child studies, even if the parent has to raise their hands at their child for that.

They try very hard so that their child never has to face a negative reaction from friends by correcting each and every behaviour when their child is interacting and playing with friends.

They may try to never let their child feel frustrated by letting them win in a game just to make them happy.

Children of such parents do not mature as they grow and become more and more dependent on their parents to save them from disappointments every time. They never learn to become resilient and responsible, and are unable to face the consequences of their actions as they grow up.

What if we let the child face the natural consequences of their actions?

Going back to the example of completing homework, consider what happens if the parent makes the decision to send the child to school without their homework completed when they refuse to do it, and let the child face the natural consequence of their actions. The parent may be sowing the first seeds of making the child responsible for their work. This may be a very hard thing for any parent to do, but when the child faces the teacher's comments in the class about their homework being incomplete, chances are that next time, the child will choose to cooperate in finishing the homework to avoid being pulled up in class. The struggle at home around completing schoolwork may reduce.

I know here, some parents may wonder: 'What if my child still doesn't want to do his homework and doesn't really care what happens in school?' The answer to this depends on how the parent chooses to handle the situation and what their attitude is while they allow the child to experience the natural consequences at school.

It matters how a parent responds

The parent's response in the following scenarios may dilute the purpose of learning from natural consequences.

• The 'told you so' response

When your child comes back from school, you say something like, 'See, I told you ma'am will ask you for the homework; that's why I tell you to do it' or 'Now you will understand you have to do your homework' instead of empathizing and being more supportive. Such words disconnect us from the child and may make them more stubborn, leading them to say, 'I don't care what the teacher says; I will not do my homework.'

What we should try to say are things like, 'Oh, everyone had done the work, you had to finish doing it in school?' and then, 'What about today? I think today you can do the work and take it tomorrow, what do you say? I can help you if you need.' Can you see the difference between the two responses? In the second instance, we offer our support while empathizing with the child's feelings instead of blaming them. Children need to feel better to do better, that is how their brain works.

- Negativity surrounding homework

When a parent nags the child excessively to complete their homework or gets angry and irritated in the process of doing it, the child loses interest in the work. They become stubborn and soon reach the point of rebelling, where they do not care anymore about completing the task or facing the negative consequences of not finishing the work. Here, the parent has to fix the negative associations that have formed with regard to homework by changing their attitude and being more patient with the task. Also, the parent must be more tolerant about how the child does the work when they actually do it. For example, if my son does not write neatly in his book, I would be okay with it and not nag him to do it differently; after all, it is his work.

- Underlying causes of the child's behaviour

There is always something underlying our children's behaviour when they are being stubborn: it may be a transition the child is facing at home, the child feeling disconnected from the parent or the child facing difficulty in school. It may also be something as simple as the child being unable to understand what is being taught and struggling to follow through with the homework as a result—perhaps, the work is too difficult for the child's age or ability. If that is the case, the parent may have to observe and see where the child needs help and make the work more manageable for them by breaking it into doable parts or by reducing the work after consulting the teacher.

- Not providing the minimum support and letting the child do it all on their own

Sometimes, when parents are first learning to let children face consequences, they move from one extreme to another. Imagine a parent leaving a child completely alone and solely responsible for doing their homework and not even asking or reminding them to do it. This response from the parent will not work in making children responsible. Children do need their parents' help in moving toward being responsible. So, we need to provide them with the minimum support required based on their stage of learning. For example, you can just remind them, 'Do you need my help in completing your work or you can do it yourself?' or encourage them with words like, 'You have become so responsible these days, you did your work on your own last time.'

Appropriate responses after a child has faced a natural consequence at school for not doing their work should look like this:

- Be kind to them and empathize with their feelings: 'Oh, that must have been awful' and 'I can see how upset you are about it.' When parents do this, they are able to connect with their children and increase the effectiveness of the lesson.

- The parent should then remind them of the lesson in a matter-of-fact way with words such as, 'I can understand, this has happened to me as well. If we don't do our work, teachers do get upset.'

- It is also helpful to ask children questions like, 'Why do you think that happened?', 'What will you do next time?' or 'Do you think I can help you in any way to avoid this the next time?'

- Then the parent can encourage the child and give them hope with words like 'I am sure you will be careful next time. This happens to the best of us.'

Here, the parent is connecting with the child and helping them see things from a broader perspective. Instead of judging them for their mistakes, the parent helps the child look at the situation as a learning opportunity.

Here, I want to share two of my several experiences of letting my child learn from natural consequences.

Experience 1: When my son, Saiveer, turned two, he picked up the habit of using the bad word 'pagal'.* In spite of my advice to the family members around me to ignore Saiveer when he used it, they paid a lot of attention to him when he said that word and this was beyond my control. In fact, they would laugh at him and even make him repeat that word as they found it really cute for a little boy to say something like that. This made the word stick in Saiveer's mind even more (as we know, behaviours we pay attention to increase in a child).

Later, when people started correcting him and telling him, 'It is a bad word, don't say it', it was of no use as Saiveer kept repeating it. Also, this word was commonly used by other family members as well at times, so it was becoming impossible to teach him to stop using it. He would even say it to shopkeepers, our helpers at home or even to his grandfather. I completely ignored Saiveer when he said 'pagal' as I knew that any attention from me was only going to increase this unwanted behaviour. I would let him know now and then, 'I know you can control not saying it, beta, as you are growing older now. Little children do not know how to control it, but you are a big boy now.'

---

* Mad.

Here, *a natural consequence helped correct my son's behaviour. A few years later, when my son was five, he and I were taking a cab from one city to another. The cab driver was an old man with a heavy build. At one point during the journey, the cab driver said something that Saiveer didn't like, and he called the elderly gentleman pagal. The driver reprimanded Saiveer for such language but my son (already irritable with the long drive) could not control repeating the word. The cab driver got extremely irritated and lashed out at my son and started shouting at me for not teaching him the right values. I remember he said, 'I am such an old man, and your son is talking like this to me and you are not even scolding him.' I had to take a deep breath. I apologized to the driver but also reminded him that my son was just a child. Witnessing the whole unfortunate episode, my son started crying and got a little scared.*

However, what came out of the whole experience is that my son learned to control saying that word and stopped using it with strangers. A lesson that I could not teach him in three years, was effectively taught when he experienced a natural consequence!

Experience 2: I had taken Saiveer to a play area when he was four years old. There, he wanted to play with an older boy, whom we didn't really know. Saiveer kept going after him and hovering over him, wanting to play with the boy, but the boy did not seem interested in playing with my son. I told Saiveer, 'I don't think he wants to play with you, let's not bother him as he does not like this.' But Saiveer did not listen and continued his efforts.

At this point, I chose to observe the situation, keeping my eye on my son the whole time. After a few minutes, the older boy got irritated and pushed my son. Saiveer was extremely upset. He came to me crying. I took him in my arms and empathized with him: 'Oh, you are upset. I saw that boy pushed you. It must have felt so bad.' I only added one line after a pause, 'When someone does not want to play with us, we cannot force them to.'

I took the opportunity of this natural consequence to give my son a small lesson about personal boundaries. What an experience teaches, explanations cannot!

Are we really letting our children experience difficult emotions?

Consider the following scenario:

You are at a park with your five-year-old and there is a balloon seller. Your child wants a balloon so you decide to buy one for them. After you pay for the balloon, you tell your child, 'Let me carry this balloon till the car as it is filled with hydrogen gas and it may fly away if we do not hold it properly.'

But your child insists on holding the balloon themselves and so you let them, with the instructions that they should be careful. You also let them know, 'We won't buy more balloons, so be careful with this one. I know you can be careful.'

Just five steps from the balloon seller, your child loses their grip on the string and the balloon floats away.

What would you do in such a situation? Would you buy another balloon for your child or would you stick to your initial decision of not buying another balloon?

If you choose to buy another balloon for your child, this is what happens:

- Instead of the child learning, 'When I am not careful, the balloon flies away; so, I need to be more careful', they learn, 'When I am not careful and the balloon flies away, my parent buys me another one.' Thus, instead of learning to be responsible, the child may learn that when they are irresponsible, their parent saves them from the consequences.

- The child also gets the message that even if the parent says that they will not buy another balloon, they do. This makes the parent's words lose value and the next time, the child does not take the parent seriously.

- Even when a parent buys another balloon, they more often than not scold the child for not being careful, thinking their words will make the child responsible more than actually letting the child experience the disappointment of losing the balloon.

When I share this example in my workshops, many parents ask me, 'Is it so wrong to buy a small thing like a balloon for the child a second time?' or 'Do we have to be so hard on our kids that we do not even give them a second chance in such a situation?'

My answer is: No, it is not entirely wrong or detrimental to buy the balloon again, nor is it likely to cause any lifelong damage to the child. The point I am trying to emphasize through the example of the balloon is that if an opportunity arises for the child to experience a natural consequence and learn from it, then it is better to take it because these opportunities are not very easy to come across, especially when they involve such low cost and pain.

Now, let me give you the perspective of what happens when we do not buy the balloon for a second time.

The child feels disappointed at the loss of the balloon they really wanted. As they feel upset, they express it by crying or some other such behaviour. For a parent handling the situation, the next ten minutes may prove to be tough. But after the feelings of disappointment in the child pass, they move on to something else. We have all seen our children become completely calm and normal right after a big meltdown ends. So, although the immediate moments following a parent's refusal to buy a balloon again may turn out to be difficult, there are some gains that will ultimately help in the long-term parenting journey.

- Once the child feels the emotion of disappointment and deals with it, they take the first step towards learning the skill of dealing with disappointments better. This sows the first seeds of resilience in them.

- The child gets the message that they themselves are responsible for their behaviour because neither the parent solved the challenge for them nor did they scold them. The parent simply lets the child experience the impact of their decision.

- The child learns from their own experience without the parent having to get angry or lecture them. The parent did not become the bad guy; in fact, they empathized with the child with words like: 'Oh, the balloon is gone, this is so sad'; 'I miss the balloon myself, this must be hard for you.' The parent shows that they understand and connect with the child's emotion and lets the consequence do the teaching.

Remember, the child may say, 'I want one more balloon'. The parent's job is to be calm and say, 'I know beta, we will buy another one next time.' When we do not get too angry but instead validate and connect with the child's feelings, they do not get too adamant. The child is able to deal with their own feelings and regulate their emotions better.

Also, remember that there may be times when the same situation may not be an opportunity to teach the child a natural consequence. For example, the child or the parent is unwell or going through a lot already; or there is another family member present who may buy the balloon even if the parent refuses to. In such cases, the parent can always assess the situation and decide to buy the balloon. We do not need to be hard on ourselves, we just need to be aware and seize the opportunity of a natural consequence when there is one.

Things to note when using natural consequences as lessons

Before parents can expect to successfully use opportunities of natural consequences as teachable moments, they must remember to build their own resilience. For parents, seeing children experience difficult emotions gets extremely uncomfortable. This is the main reason that they tend to give in when children throw tantrums or try to find ways to solve difficult situations, just so that the child doesn't have to experience unpleasant emotions. But we forget that in order to become emotionally resilient and learn how to accept failures, disappointments and frustrations in life, they have to experience these feelings and learn to deal with them.

In the experiences I shared with you above, it was not easy for me to let my child go through unpleasant situations—it was hard to watch him get pushed into the play area by an older child. I could have chosen to become very strict with my son, watching him and correcting him every time he got closer to the older boy—this would probably have saved him from being pushed by the other child. But then how would Saiveer have learnt about how different children may behave in various ways in different situations? I could have been angry with my son for using the bad word 'pagal' in the cab to satisfy the driver's ego, but then, how would my son have learnt that people get offended by such words? This was especially so because, at home, no family member was reacting negatively to him using that word and my anger seemed to have had no effect on Saiveer's use of the word for years.

I want to highlight two more points to clarify my point further:

- I do have my child's back and I do not abandon him completely even when I let him experience the natural consequences of his behaviour. In fact, I am emotionally available to support my son when he experiences difficult situations. Of course, I will not hesitate to step in and save him in situations that may be detrimental to his mental and physical health. Parents must judge the consequences that children may face based on their age and the damage that the situation can cause.

- It is not that because I allow my son to experience the effect of his behaviour, I do not inform him about the wrong behaviours or their consequences. I did tell him 'pagal' is a bad word to use or the boy did not want to play with him. But if Saiveer chooses not to listen to me, I let him experience the situation and the resultant effects when I can, so that he gets the message by experiencing it first-hand, especially when I am around and can oversee the situation so that it does not get out of control.

To reiterate the point I made earlier: children need to go through certain consequences in order to mature. The more we overprotect our children, the more we delay their maturity.

We must also remember that as children grow, the consequences of their actions become more and more severe and detrimental. Let me explain this by asking you this: Are the negative consequences more severe and detrimental in the case of a two-year-old child's negative behaviour or a fifteen-year-old child's?

The obvious answer is that a fifteen-year-old child's irresponsible behaviour is going to cost much more than a two-year-old's. After all, a fifteen-year-old makes many decisions independently and we cannot control their actions to a very large extent. They may get into detrimental situations like falling prey to drug abuse, being in car accidents or having unprotected sex. A two-year-old is still more or less always around us and the repercussions of their actions are often not as life-threatening.

If parents allow children to learn through consequences while they are younger when the effects of their actions are less painful, children grow up to become more mature and responsible for their actions and behaviour. Parents think children should not make mistakes, but they forget that in that case, children do not learn from them either. In fact, sometimes parents say, 'I don't want my child to make the mistakes that I have made.' But children cannot learn from their parents' mistakes—they must learn from their own, and parents must give them the space to learn.

It will never be pleasant for parents when their kids mess up, but children will always learn something from their mistakes if parents handle the situations in the right way. I hope this chapter helps you in getting a wider perspective on how facing consequences are more helpful than we ever thought. Next time when you face a difficult situation because of your child's action, always remember, 'My child is learning something from this. I simply need to do my part and be patient for my child to become more mature through these experiences.'

In the next chapter, I will discuss how sometimes, we have to set up consequences for our children's actions, especially when we cannot wait for natural consequences to occur.

15

Artificial Consequences

Now that we clearly understand what we mean by consequences, it is time to learn how we can use artificial consequences with our children to discipline them. As the name suggests, these are consequences that are not natural but created by us for disciplining problematic behaviours. These should be used when parents have applied all the points mentioned under 'positive discipline' in Section 4 but are still not getting the child's cooperation, and when it is not feasible to wait for natural consequences to occur.

To clarify further, let's take the example of a three-year-old hitting. We understand that children experiment with hitting at this age but we still have to stop them as we cannot allow them to hit. In a situation where a child is hitting another child and is unable to control their hands even after the parent has validated the child's emotions at that moment and has firmly put a boundary in place, the parent may need to put a consequence in place to help the child control their actions.

Now, let's consider a six-year-old who refuses to complete his studies every day. If a child does not do their everyday work, parents can help by forming a routine, empathizing with them, checking for unrealistic expectations placed on the child, keeping their patience and being more encouraging. But in spite of doing everything, if the child refuses to cooperate and the struggle with studies continues, then perhaps a simple consequence can help in gaining the child's cooperation.

Most parents have faced such situations. After all, we are dealing with the still-developing brains of children. As we know, very young children lack regulation and are impulsive—they haven't yet mastered the skill of sound decision-making and are unable to see the implications of their own behaviours. So they need help in maintaining boundaries. Setting up artificial consequences is a technique which helps with that.

Implementing artificial consequences

An artificial consequence is a result that follows a child's behaviour that their parents want to discipline. But these consequences must not be treated as punishments or threats. A simple artificial consequence, if a child hits other children, can be that they are removed from the area and not allowed to play for a few minutes.

Similarly, when a child does not do their everyday work, a simple artificial consequence for them could be that they are unable to watch screens for that day.

Setting up an artificial consequence is a technique involving five crucial steps. I refer to it as a formula where each and every step is equally important. If a single step is missed, parents will not get an effective result because then the entire technique is affected.

Before I explain the five steps, let us look at two example situations that will then help us explain and clarify each step. These are common situations parents face at home with children:

Situation 1: You live in a joint family and there are many children in the house who play together. Your four-year-old has started hitting his cousins while playing. And when that happens, you are called to sort out your child's behaviour. You have tried to explain to your child many times that 'we cannot hit', 'hands are not for hitting' and 'we need to be gentle'. You have also used empathy and validation but the little underdeveloped prefrontal cortex in your child's brain is unable to regulate the behaviour of hitting. As a parent, you cannot allow your child to hit.

Situation 2: You want to practise reading and writing with your six-year-old every day. You have fixed a time for the task and have kept the expectations realistic by making the tasks short, simple and not too complicated for your child. You have tried being extra patient by using a respectful tone and empathizing with your child whenever they express that the work is boring. But still, you are struggling and your child is not cooperating with you on most days in doing their reading and writing practice.

How do we use artificial consequences in the above scenarios? We follow the steps of the formula I am detailing here.

1. We inform the child of the consequences before the behaviour happens

The first rule of having a consequence in place is that the child should be pre-informed about it, which means that the child should know the consequence (or what will happen) before they indulge in the unwanted behaviour. There is no sudden rule formed or decision taken. This point is necessary because consequences are basically **options** that the child chooses through their behaviours—they can either choose to indulge in a behaviour and go through the consequence set for it or they can choose to control their behaviour and avoid the consequence. However, the child can only choose if the consequence is communicated to them beforehand.

Let's see how this can be applied in the case of the first example where the child is hitting their cousins.

Here, we can set up the consequence that every time the child hits a cousin, the child is taken back to their room for some time. The lesson we are trying to communicate to the child is that we cannot hurt others and if we do behave in a way that hurts others, we cannot play with them. We can inform the child of the consequence of being taken back to their room and missing playtime before they go to play with their cousins, maybe when we are getting them ready for the day. Once the child knows what is going to happen as a result of their behaviour, they can either choose to control their hands and play with their cousins or they can choose to hit and lose playtime with the cousins. This makes the child responsible for their own behaviour.

Now let us look at example situation 2 where the child does not cooperate in completing the practice work set for them.

Here, we can set up the simple consequence of losing screen time of the day when practice work is not done. The lesson that we want to communicate to the child is that we all complete our work and then have a fun time. We want the child to know that just as Mom and Dad complete their work and then relax and indulge in leisure activities, the same applies to the child. We inform the child of the consequences before we start the practice work. As the child knows what to expect, they can choose from two options: they can either complete their work and enjoy screen time or they don't complete the work and miss screen time for the day. The ball is in the child's court.

Remember, when we give options to children as in the above situations, we have to be prepared for the child to take either of the options. This means that even if the child takes the option of going through the consequences, we need to be okay with it and keep our calm. It is most likely that the child will experiment with the boundary and test if their parents keep their word about implementing the consequence. They may have to go through experiencing the consequences a couple of times before they start being more responsible. Also, when they do face the repercussions of their decision, parents must empathize and keep encouraging them to take the better option the next time. The next steps will help you understand what I mean here.

2. There is no anger when we communicate the consequences

When we communicate a boundary and the consequences we have set up to the child, we need to make sure that we are not angry. We must be calm and matter-of-fact about it, and the tone and words we use should make them feel that we are still in their team, with the consequence being something that both the parent and the child need to follow. Let's see how we do this in our example situations.

Situation 1:
While getting the child ready in the room (after which they are going to leave the room and play with everyone), we connect with the child and inform them of the consequences politely and lovingly. We can use

the following words. Note that after every line, there is a pause and a response from the child:

'*You are ready now and you will go and play with everyone. Are you excited?*'

'*But remember we have to control our hands. We cannot hit.*'

'*If you hit then I will* **have to** *get you back to the room. Then you* **will not be able to** *play with them for some time.*'

'*I don't want to get you back to the room, but I cannot let you hit. I think you can control your hands though okay.*' (*A high five can end the conversation.*)

Situation 2:

'*We will do our work now, I know you can do it very fast.*'

'*After work, it will be time for you to watch your tablet. But we can only watch the screen if we complete our work and I really want you to enjoy the screen.*'

If the child still refuses to do the work, we say, '*Then we will* **not be able to** *have screen time today; I hope you are okay with it. Because I really want you to watch it, my darling.*'

We stay calm and say, '*I know you want to. Let me help you and we will complete this small task. You can do it, I know you can choose to watch the screen. We all need to practise to get good at things, bacha.*'

Now, we let the child decide what option they want to take. Remember, we have to be okay with them choosing either option without losing our calm. What

we are trying to achieve here is long-term cooperation—
we need our children to become more responsible for
their work instead of us becoming responsible for
their work. The consequences are simply a way to
help the child make the decision to do their work on
their own without us yelling at or threatening them.
Consequences are not threats but simple rules that we
set up calmly and with kindness, which help us and
also let the child know that we are in their team.

We can also use the 'bug theory' here to help the
child, which I will explain later in the chapter.

A few things to keep in mind when implementing
this step:

a. Our tone while informing the consequence is calm,
respectful and firm.

b. We use phrases like 'I will **have to**', and 'I **don't
want to**'. This makes the consequence look like a
firm boundary and not a threat. A threat will sound
more like this: 'If you hit, then I will bring you back
to the room and not let you play with anyone' or
'If you don't do the work, I will not give you the
tab!' These words make it sound like we are using
our power over them. Instead, we need to make
sure the child knows that we are on their side and
the consequence is something external that we need
to follow.

c. We must make sure that our words encourage the
child and communicate that they do not necessarily
have to go through the consequences if they choose

to. We do this by using words like, 'You can control your hands' or 'You can complete the work'. We show confidence in the child and do not put them down with words like 'You always hit when you play' or 'You never do your work on your own'.

d. We use fewer words with young kids so as to make sure they understand what we are saying instead of getting lost in too many words. You can even say it in short: 'If you hit, back to the room, okay?' or 'You can control your hands' and then give a high five. Even in the second situation, after the conversation, be careful not to indulge in an argument with the child by repeating the lines again and again. Be calm and use a few words, giving the child space to make their own decision.

Thus, a respectful tone expressing confidence in your child, without conveying irritation or sounding like a threat, is the second ingredient of setting up artificial consequences.

3. We only set up consequences that we can follow through

As I mentioned before, consequences are options for children to choose from. And when we give them such options, as parents we need to be prepared for them to choose either of the options.

While setting up consequences, we must always remember: We cannot control our children's behaviour or the options that they decide to take. We focus on what we can control instead of getting irritated with our children's choices. Thus, we only use consequences that we can control and follow through because children will test the boundaries. If we set a boundary that we cannot follow, the child will stop taking our words seriously and the consequence will turn into an empty threat. It is better to not set up a consequence at all than to use one that we cannot follow through with.

For example, the consequence of bringing the child back to the room in case of unwanted behaviour will not work in the case of an older child because we cannot pick them up physically and bring them back. In case the child says, 'I will not go to the room', we will become helpless and feel that consequences do not work. And if we end up arguing with the child about going to the room, then the actual lesson takes a backseat and there develops an additional issue that needs to be solved.

In the second situation, when we set up the consequence of no screen time, we must make sure that we have control of all the screens. Sometimes parents say, 'But then my child switches on the television and starts watching, what can I do?' Firstly, it is wise to have screen controls as much as possible and for as long as possible as we all understand the negative effects of screens and want to avoid them. Secondly, if you don't control the screens, then it's better not to have 'no screen time' as a consequence at all. It is essential to remember what we have control over and then create artificial consequences based on that.

Also, as far as possible, we should try to set up a consequence that is related to the unwanted behaviour. In the first situation, we are considering that 'going back to the room' is related to hitting the cousins—the consequence is physically removing the child by taking them away and giving them space, as we cannot allow the child to hit.

4. **We connect with our children through calm and empathy while implementing the consequences**

Whenever we have to follow through with a consequence, chances are that the child is not going to like it and will throw some kind of tantrum. We need to anticipate such behaviours so that we do not get intimidated by them. After all, we understand that consequences are not fun for children to face. So it is only natural that children will feel some emotions and will express them in their behaviour.

An important point I want to reinforce here is that we are disciplining the child's behaviour and not their feelings. Children should be allowed to express what they feel without judgement and also be given space to express their emotions in ways that are not harmful (like crying, whining, complaining and yelling). These feelings will ultimately pass—our job as parents is to maintain our connection with the child through calmness and empathy so that they know that we are on their team, even when the consequence is intact and in place. We do not need to get angry to follow through with a consequence, we just need to do what we have decided upon.

Let us see what this looks like in our examples.

Situation 1:

After the child leaves their room and joins their cousins, we wait for the child to hit at some point. The minute that happens, we go to the child and say something like, 'Oh ho, you were not able to control your hands. Now we will have to go back to the room, my bacha.' Here, your child will express in their words and behaviour that they don't want to go. He may say, 'I will not hit now; no I don't want to go' and start crying or get angry.

It is important to take deep breaths here and not get triggered. Empathize with the child and say, 'I know sweetheart, I know you don't want to', and lay the boundary, 'But we have to, so I will pick you up and we are going back to the room for some time.'

In case family members say, 'It's okay, don't do that', we should calmly respond, 'I know, we just need a few minutes, we will be back very soon.' We must be kind and firm while maintaining a calm body and mind. Then we take the child back to the room even if it seems a little dramatic.

Once we reach the room, the child may continue crying and throw a tantrum. We should allow the child to let their emotions out while showing empathy both in words and behaviour. We may say 'I know', 'We cannot hit', 'I wish I didn't have to get you' and 'I love you, my baby'. You may choose to say anything that suits the situation. Also, in case the child struggles to go out of the room, gently lock the room and say, 'We will go out in just ten minutes. I want to take you out too. But right now, I think you need me.'

We must be very calm and loving in spite of the child's behaviour and our body's vibration also needs to be positive. We need to be in control of our behaviour because the minute we lose it, we lose control of the situation.

Once the child calms down, we hug them and let them go back out to play. And before we leave the room, we remind the child of the consequence again: 'You can play now, I am so happy about it. But remember, control your hands. I do not want to get you back, I know you can control yourself.' Maybe end the talk with another high five and let your child leave.

I hope you can see by now, how consequences act as options from which children can choose. In our example, we have given the child the choice either to control their hands and continue playing or to hit others and go back to the room. After all, we need our children to control their hands and not hit even when we are not around, and that can only happen when the children are themselves motivated to control their own behaviour and practise self-regulation. Setting up the consequence of going back to the room is just a way to help them choose the right behaviour while being kind.

Let us look at situation 2:

After we tell the child to do the work in a positive way and inform them of their options, and still the child decides not to complete their task, we remain calm and let the day pass. When the child asks for the screen, we maintain our calm and say, 'I wish I could give the tab to you, but we had to complete our practice before that.' Here, the child may either throw a tantrum or may say, 'I will do the work now.'

In the former situation, we let the tantrum pass without giving the screen to them. We may say, 'I am sure you can watch it tomorrow. I think you can do the work and win tomorrow' so that they are encouraged for the next day instead of arguing on and on about the same day. Remember, it is important for us to not attach too much importance to that particular day's work and keep the long-term objective in mind. In case we get angry or get into an argument, the technique will not work. The only thing we need to follow for that day is 'no screen time' so that the child understands the boundary will be followed and makes better decisions the next day. We must be careful not to nag the child the whole day about not doing the work. Let the child process it on his own.

If the child offers to do the work to win screen time, it is always better to give them a chance to redeem themselves. This helps them gain confidence that they can easily complete their everyday work and enjoy the screen without any struggle. We may also say, 'You did

it, you won over your bug!' (I will shortly tell you the
'bug theory'.)

 With time, more than a consequence, this becomes
a routine for the child. Of course, parents should
expect some days to be smoother than others.

5. We consistently follow the consequences

When we set up a consequence, we consistently follow
through every time the unwanted behaviour takes
place. If we are inconsistent, that is, if we sometimes
allow the behaviour to happen and we don't enforce
the consequence, the children then take the situation
lightly and start testing us more to see what they can
get away with. That is why it is all the more important
to thoughtfully choose a consequence that is easy to
follow through consistently.

 There are two things that parents ought to keep in
mind here:

a. First, parents should maintain an attitude where
 they encourage the child to save themselves from the
 consequences. It is important to show them that we
 are on their side trying to help them. Parents must
 also maintain a connection with the child by being
 calm and empathizing with them when required.
 For example, in the first situation, where we are
 trying to discourage the child from hitting, we may
 remind and encourage the child while they are
 playing with words like 'You are playing so well.

I knew you could do it.' In case they are about to hit, you can nudge and remind them, 'You can control it. You did it!'

You can try to use the bug theory that I came up with for my son, which not only helped me to communicate a consequence in a positive way but also helped me encourage him to save himself from the consequence.

The bug theory

The bug theory simply says that there is a bug in all of us that wants us to go through an uncomfortable consequence. This bug does not want us to enjoy ourselves. But we can all win against that bug using our will and self-control. When we win against the bug, we choose the behaviour that is more advantageous for us and save ourselves from the negative consequences.

For example, we can choose to win against the bug by completing our work on time and then we can enjoy by watching the screen. It is also important that we let children know that we all, both adults and children, have this bug. Sometimes, in appropriate situations, I even say, 'My bug won today baby, I didn't want to shout like that. I will breathe and win against it from now on.'

In the case of the second example situation, this is how I communicated this theory to my four-year-old:

'*I want you to watch the screen, but there is a bug inside you that does not want you to watch and enjoy. You will have to win against the bug. Tell your bug, "I will watch the screen, I will do the work, I can do it." I know you can win, my child.*'
In case his bug does win, that is, he is unable to do his work and he does lose his screen time, instead of blaming my child, I blame the bug.

'*The bug won this time, beta. It's okay. You can win tomorrow and watch the screen tomorrow. I will help you in winning over the bug.*'
I remember one day my son cried saying, 'Why did the bug win, mamma? I wanted to win.' I said to him, 'It's okay, beta. It happens sometimes with everyone. You can win next time, I am here for you.' This helped him make peace with his mistakes. He still went through the consequences, but he knew he had my love and support through it.
This theory helps children:

- To believe in their inner goodness and encourage them to change their ways the next time instead of making them stubborn. Knowing that everyone has this bug helps them feel that they are not bad and that there is nothing wrong with them.
- To understand the concept of self-control in concrete terms, which enables them to practise controlling their behaviour and impulses.
- To become more resilient as they face the consequences as well as the associated emotions

and still feel empowered that they can win against their bug the next time.

b. Second, that things may not always go as planned. Even though consistency is important, it does not mean being hard on ourselves as parents if we are unable to do what we planned.

- There may be times when you set up a consequence but later realize that it would not be feasible to carry through. This is completely fine, as we can change things the next time. We are also learning and growing as parents.

- There may be times when a consequence that was working until a certain point stops being effective. Remember, children are also changing as they grow. In such a situation, it is time to change the consequences and understand the child's growing needs.

- There may be times when someone overrides your decision to implement a consequence. This may be your own spouse or another family member. Here, instead of getting irritated or arguing with the family member in front of the child, breathe and think of better ways to deal with the situation or surrender in that instance; you can talk to the other adult later, when the child is not around, to gain their cooperation.

Once, I decided that my son would not get the tab, but he ended up watching the screen because someone else gave it to him. Here, I had a choice: I could implement the consequence the next day by saying, 'You can watch the screen now, but we will skip tomorrow instead of today.' This prevents turning the situation into an issue because there is nothing much I can do at the moment and I want to avoid a power struggle.

Whenever such a scenario occurred at home, where the rule I implemented was overridden by someone else, I would honestly communicate to my son, 'I don't want to fight for the TV now, so I will skip tomorrow's movie time instead. It is your choice what you want to skip.' I reminded myself that I could not control my son's access to the TV at that instant, but I could control movie time in the future. So I maintained my calm and made sure that my tone was kind and not threatening.

In such cases, I have found that my son sometimes says, 'I don't want to miss tomorrow's movie time' and switches off the TV instantly. This happens because I am not angry and because he knows that the next day, I will follow through with what I just said.

If he chooses to switch the TV off, I reinforce my connection with him at that instant and say, 'I am so proud of you, I knew you could do it' and also engage in more positive interactions.

If, however, this does not happen and my son chooses to watch the TV, I continue with my day by reminding myself of my long-term parenting goals and choose not to take one scenario too personally. I also try to plan things better the next time while continuing to work on my connection with my child. **'I cannot control my child's behaviour but I can control mine' is the mantra that helps me the most.**

Consequences are most effective when we implement them remembering what we can control, when we are calm and firm, and when we make maintaining the connection with our child our priority without taking things personally. But there will be times when we may feel that consequences are not working. So, let's see what happens that makes consequences fail.

When do consequences not work?

- *When we get angry or irritated:* One of the most important rules to keep in mind is to not let our emotions take over. The technique of setting up consequences is extremely effective but consequences are not very easy to follow consistently. When children test our patience or throw tantrums, it becomes very difficult to maintain a calm body and mind; it also becomes challenging to maintain our connection. But the minute we get angry, the consequence turns into a threat or punishment. This makes the child dysregulated and we do not achieve the desired result. To be in control of implementing a consequence, we only need to apply it without getting angry—sounds easy, but in reality, it needs a lot of patience and practice.

- *When we do not empathize and only place a boundary:* Validating our children's emotions even when we are setting up a boundary helps us better communicate the end goal to children. For example, when a child hits someone and their parents say, 'No hitting' or 'Hitting is bad, say sorry', they are just setting up a boundary without connecting with the child. To bring empathy to their words, parents can say, 'I can see you got upset, but we can't hit' or 'I think you are hungry so you are unable to control yourself, but we still cannot hit. We will stop playing now and eat something first.' When we validate the emotions or the underlying need causing the child's actions, they feel more understood and this increases the chances of them cooperating with us not only in the moment but also in the long run.

- *When there already exists a disconnection in the relationship:* When we use the technique of setting up consequences in a relationship that, in general, lacks connection, the chances are that the technique will not work. Remember, one of the fundamental elements of positive discipline is connection. When we have too many negative interactions with our children in the form of showing them a lack of patience or anger, using threats or engaging in an existing power struggle, then chances are that children will rebel or completely break down when faced with a consequence. Thus, it is important that we first work on the relationship in general (you can read the section on connection again for ways to do that). If we want our children to behave better, we ourselves need to model better behaviour first.

- *When we are not addressing the underlying cause of the behaviour that we are trying to discipline using consequences:* There is always a deeper reason underlying our children's behaviour. If a child is giving their parents a hard time in doing some work, there may be underlying reasons such as, they are finding the work too hard, the parent is easily losing patience during the work or the child is too exhausted by the time they start doing the work and so on. Before and even while setting up consequences, parents need to keep trying to understand what could be behind their children's non-cooperation. If instead of trying to understand the cause of our children's behaviour, we directly jump to the step of setting up consequences, the technique will certainly not work.

- *When our expectation from the child is unrealistic:* Parents must make sure that their child is capable of the behaviour that is being expected from them in terms of their age and temperament. For example, it is futile to expect a two-year-old to sit for thirty minutes in one place to complete an activity. Setting up a consequence if the child is unable to meet this expectation will not work, because at this age the child's brain is not at the developmental stage where they can focus for so long. Thus, no matter how many consequences you keep, they will not work to encourage the child in that behaviour.

- *When we use too many artificial consequences:* Consequences are effective when they are used sparingly. When consequences are used frequently to get the child to cooperate, they may start feeling too controlled and may even start rebelling. Also, if consequences have to be used by parents too often, it is a symptom that their relationship with the child lacks connection—instead of using consequences, the parents first need to work on building the parent–child connection.

- *When we try to discipline emotions:* Some parents set up consequences if their children cry, shout or argue. Please understand that emotions must not be disciplined, and behaviours such as crying and shouting happen because the child is overwhelmed with emotions. We need to give space to our children to let their feelings out in some ways, especially the ones that are not harmful. Such threats must be avoided: 'Stop crying or else I will not give the chocolate.' Also, keep in mind that children cannot behave according to our expectations all the time. It is essential that we accept that children will be children and not discipline every behaviour that we find uncomfortable. Remember, we need to always choose our battles.

- *When it is not an appropriate consequence:* If the consequence that we have set up is not important enough and does not affect the child much, they are more than okay to go through it. The child has to want to avoid the consequences and be motivated enough to regulate their behaviour.

Additionally, when the duration or intensity of the consequence is too much, the child may feel completely hopeless and demotivated. For example, taking away screen time for a whole month. Here the child may give up trying to correct their behaviour as they feel demotivated and the whole point of the consequence is lost. In fact, consequences should be simple so that the child gets a chance to redeem themselves with better behaviour, which is the main purpose of using this technique.

Let me share a few examples of the consequences of not working with my son.

When Saiveer was three and a half, I enrolled him in a class where he had to practise numbers by using small booklets every day. These practise booklets of ten pages each were very easy to do and hardly took three to five minutes to complete. Many of his friends of the same age were learning very well in the class and that motivated me to enrol my son for it as well.

Within the first two days of Saiveer starting to do the work with my help, he began refusing to do the booklets. So, I tried to set up the artificial consequence of no screen time if the booklet was not completed and followed all the steps we discussed earlier. However, I still failed to gain his cooperation and also started losing my patience around the task. At one point, he did not want to do the worksheets at all and was okay with losing screen time for it. This completely dissolved my purpose. I had to sit back and reflect on what was not working:

1. *My expectations were unrealistic and I was not exploring the underlying cause of Saiveer's behaviour. The reason my son was not able to do the worksheet was that he was different from other children; it was harder for him to sit and focus to complete the ten-page booklet in one go. He was not yet capable of doing what I expected of him.*

2. *I had started losing my patience and was not calm even if I was quiet, which made me disconnected from my child. This is the most common error that we tend to make when setting up consequences. My anger and irritation made him rebel and he lost the motivation to do the work.*

I took a few steps to rectify the situation: First, I discontinued the classes for a few days to rebuild my connection with my son and also to break the negative association formed with doing the booklets. Second, when I restarted the classes after a month, instead of doing all ten pages at one go, I only worked on three pages with my son on the first day. This made him feel that he could do the work without getting too harassed about completing the booklet. It took us almost twenty days to build up momentum so that Saiveer could complete the entire booklet in one sitting. I had to remember to form a positive association regarding the work by being patient and making the process fun with my behaviour. Third, though my son started doing the booklets, with time, I realized that they were not as useful for my son as for other children considering Saiveer's unique temperament; I finally discontinued the classes altogether after a couple of months.

I hope this gives you a practical example of how and when consequences may not work as well as why it is important to understand our children and not plainly set up consequences to discipline them.

Natural consequences are always better than artificial consequences

Though it is hard for parents to see their children go through natural consequences, we must remember that when we have the option, it is always better to choose natural consequences over setting up artificial ones. Here's why:

1. They are more effective as these consequences are more real and based on real life. They make more sense to children, making them more resilient and helping them understand the dynamics of life better.

2. They help parents as they do not have to be the bad guys. When we set artificial consequences, there is a chance we will still be seen as the bad guy and a disconnect will crop up even if we are not angry. A natural consequence is an opportunity for the

child to learn a lesson without us doing much. In fact, we have to simply witness the situation and be supportive of our children; the learning happens on its own.

3. As I mentioned before, we should not overuse artificial consequences if we want them to be effective. When we choose a natural consequence over an artificial one, we can save the artificial one for a later time.

VI

A FEW IMPORTANT
PARENTING ISSUES

In this section, I will talk about the three most common concerns of parents: managing children around screens, helping children study better and raising children in joint families. Many of the personal sessions I have with parents revolve around these topics. So, I want to share some relevant and practical tips—keeping the information provided in the book as the basis of our parenting journey—that may help parents navigate these challenges in the most effective ways.

16

Children and Screens

The world of today in which we are all raising our children, is one of screens. Though it is obvious that screens have brought many advantages to modern life, the time spent glued to screens and the adverse effects of that are just as important matters to consider. Parents especially have many concerns around them and they often struggle with the following specific issues:

- Limiting screen time: We as parents struggle to manage the amount of time children spend engaging with screens, be it on a phone, tablet, computer or TV. We understand that too much screen time is not good for children, but whenever we take away screens from our children or limit the duration of their screen time, we face opposition from them in the form of tantrums through crying, being angry, getting into arguments and so on.

- Ensuring children's safety: Exposing our children to the world of screens is also a safety issue because of the low-quality content, addictive online games, cybercrimes and cyberbullying that are rampant in the virtual world. The amount of time spent on screens and the quality of content that children are exposed to affects their developing brains. Excessive screen exposure may lead to low attention spans, loss of creativity and behavioural issues like aggression in our children.

- Preventing screen addiction: We know how addictive screens can be and we have all heard about children who have fallen prey to screen addiction, which has taken a toll on their mental and physical health. As parents, we need to learn ways to constantly maintain a balance between preventing screen addiction, while at the same time giving children access to screens.

Keeping in mind these concerns, let us discuss some ideas that may help in this area of parenting:

1. Having clear boundaries about how much screen time the child gets and when

Many parents give their children access to screens at random times of the day without following a set routine. The first step in moving towards smoother screen time management is to sit back and decide: How much screen do I want to give to my child and when do I want to give it? Having clarity on this helps us in the following ways:

a. When we have clarity, we are not confused about when to allow our children screen time.

b. When children do ask for screen time at other times of the day, instead of only saying no or giving in because of a tantrum, we can let them know when they can use screens.

c. We can keep track of how much time our children are spending on screens and that can help us regulate the duration better.

d. With time, the child too gets used to the routine and the struggle around managing screen time reduces as they know what to expect.

For example, a parent can decide that they want their child to have one hour of screen time. The parent can then decide to give the child thirty minutes of screen time in the afternoon and thirty minutes after they come back from the playground.

Remember, the routine can be set according to our own convenience as well: for example, a parent can give the child access to the screen in the afternoon so that they can get some rest along with the child; screen time can be set during the hours the parent has work and meetings; the parent can allow screens when they need some quiet time to do some work or a parent can even allow screen time if they want to watch something together with their child. (Please note that screens should be avoided for children below two years of age.)

2. Being prepared for the struggle

When we deny our children screens, it is likely that we will face some kind of tantrum. If we anticipate these tantrums, we are less likely to get irritated and lose our calm.

Why do we face these situations?

- When we say no to our children when they really want to watch something or when we take back the screen when they are really engrossed, they do not like it and they feel the emotions of anger, frustration or helplessness. We now know that when children feel these emotions, they show them through their bodies as is normal for that stage of their brain development. Therefore, some tantrums are inevitable in these situations, and knowing that is useful for parents.
- Sometimes children realize that their behaviours of crying, shouting or arguing help them in getting their demands fulfilled. Thus, they engage in these behaviours to get more screen time as well. Even when we have formed a routine, children may test boundaries by indulging in these behaviours. When parents are consistent in their decisions and routines and maintain patience, children gradually understand that these behaviours will not work for them.

Also, remember that whenever there is a shift in children's routines—due to holidays or travel—the pattern may break for a short time and children may end up watching more screens than usual and at different times of the day. When parents try to return to the routine after the break, they must be prepared to face some struggle in the initial days as the child's brain needs time to go back to the same structure—this is because, during the break in routine their brains had gotten used to increased screen time. Once the routine is settled again and the child is used to it, things get smoother again.

3. Handling tantrums around screen time

Remember, screens are very interesting and it is only natural for children to want to watch more of them—it happens to all of us. Children may want more screen time, but that is not the real problem. The struggle arises because we cannot allow more of it and must regulate children's screen usage. So, instead of getting irritated by children's tantrums around screen usage, we need to learn to be calm, empathize and maintain the boundaries respectfully. We need to follow this formula every time our child comes to us to ask for more screen time during different times of the day.

Additionally, we must be careful about not repeating explanations during every tantrum about how screens are not good for our eyes or how they had promised they would give back the screen in thirty minutes and the time was over. Most probably, we have already used these arguments many times and repeating them will only increase the intensity or duration of the tantrum (we have already discussed this in the first section of the book).

Instead, we can just say, 'I know you want to watch this. I wish I could give you more time, but I cannot do that.' In case they continue crying, shouting or arguing, we let them feel their emotions without engaging with the behaviour. Our job is to keep the boundary intact calmly, and we do not need to get angry at them for what they want.

When we are consistent, children gradually do get the idea that tantrums will not help them change their parents' minds. Slowly tantrums around screen time start to become more and more manageable.

4. Screens should be allowed happily and taken back happily

It is important that we do not associate negativity with screens. Here, I suggest to parents that while allowing their children screens, they should have a calm and pleasant approach. To do this, parents must give up any guilt they feel around letting the child watch the screen; instead, they simply need to be conscious and mindful around screens.

Children enjoy watching screens, so we should be happy with their happiness. We can use words like, 'Yay, time to watch your favourite show now' or when they come to ask for it, we can say, 'Of course, you can watch now', instead of saying things like 'Okay watch, but not too much' or 'You only want to watch screens the whole day'. In fact, sometimes we can connect with our children by enjoying screens together. That way, we can expose them to quality content and also reduce the negative interactions around screens.

When we become too negative and keep fighting with our children about screen time, screens automatically become more enticing for them. It's like we are always pulling from one end, and so our children are pulling from the other end. So, the solution is to stick to the routine as much as possible and give access to screens with positivity and take back the screen peacefully even if the child is not peaceful about it

I remember that when I shared these ideas with one of my clients who had a ten-year-old, she had expressed, 'I was always concerned that my child gets too angry when I tell him to stop playing the game. But I realized that if I do not react and just take back the screen, the anger fades away and he is fine after a while.' Thus, our response matters very much in such situations.

5. It is okay for children to get bored

One big reason we give our children screens is that we don't want them to get bored. What we have to understand is that it is not our responsibility to solve our children's boredom all the time. Sometimes, it is important for them to get bored as it gives them a chance to be more creative and think out of the box so that they can keep themselves engaged.

Children who spend too much time watching screens and do not have enough free time are unable to find ways to entertain themselves when they need to. They start depending on the screen at all times to keep themselves busy as their brains shut down and they lose interest in other activities which they earlier found interesting. Excessive screen time also affects our children's behaviour. They may become more aggressive or passive and also may throw more tantrums around getting screen time because they get more and more addicted to it.

Thus, instead of giving children screens when they start to get bored, put in place a routine and stick to it. When you travel, it is a good idea to carry books or toys that children can play with so that we do not have to depend on screens every time to keep them busy.

6. Quality over quantity

The quality of what our children are watching and how they are consuming screens is more important than the time they spend on screens. A child passively watching videos on screens and a child learning to perhaps draw something or craft something with the help of videos are completely different scenarios.

In our current world, it is wise to empower children by teaching them how they can take advantage of screens, instead of allowing for a situation where screens end up taking advantage of them. We can do this by letting children know how they can make use of screens in ways that are appropriate for their age. For example, learning to dance, learning new easy recipes to try, enrolling for online courses and so on—depending on the age of the child.

So instead of obsessing over quantity, let us also focus on the quality of our children's screen time. Two hours of learning something online and two hours of watching videos mindlessly are definitely not the same.

7. Be more involved and keep a watch

We understand the risks of the world of internet today and thus, we need to be watchful of what our children are consuming via screens. We need to be careful when giving children independent access to phones and gadgets, where low-quality and inappropriate content is very easily accessible. Thus, putting restrictions, using passwords and setting up parental controls become extremely essential.

Being involved and showing interest in what our children are doing online when they are little is a good way to ensure our children's safety. When children want to show us a video that they find interesting or a game they are really enjoying, we must listen to them and ask questions to show curiosity instead of ignoring them. If we don't take an interest in what they have to say when they come to us, they may stop sharing what they are watching and that may become risky, especially as they grow older.

Even enjoying a game or video with our children is a good idea for parents to keep the channels of communication open around screens. We need this connection with them so that we are more informed about what they are doing. Remember, their connection with the screen increases when the connection with us decreases. Think about it.

8. Screen time limit changes with age

As children get older, their requirements for screens may change. For example, they may want to play a game online when some other friends are available to play with them, and so the pre-decided screen time we set for our child may not suit them anymore. At any point, if we feel that the rules we have formed around screens are not working anymore, it is time to reflect on the situation and change these. As children grow older, we can discuss the boundaries with them and re-frame those boundaries. This also gives children a chance to form their own boundaries around screens, and learn to regulate themselves and their screen usage before they get independent access to their own phones or gadgets when they grow older.

I would like to suggest here that in my opinion, it is wise to give personal phones with complete media access to children as late as possible. Our children's brains are developing as they grow. Their prefrontal cortex, which is responsible for making them more mature, develops slowly with age. It is better that by the time they get free access to a screen of their own, their brains are more mature so that they can make informed decisions to keep themselves safe.

17

Children and Studies

Helping children study better and reducing our struggles around studies

A common parenting challenge that I come across when interacting with parents is making children study. Here are some insights I have gathered that may help in reducing struggles around studies and make the process smoother:

1. *Do not get too anxious and stressed out around studies:* Children are most likely to lose interest in studies when their parent starts becoming impatient and irritated with matters related to it. Children may find studies interesting or boring, which depends on the child and the way they are being taught. But it is when anger and stress get associated during the time of studies that the child becomes extremely negative about the process and

starts giving us a really hard time in even sitting down to complete schoolwork (because the fact is that we are giving them a hard time as well).

It is generally our stress that becomes a barrier to our child's learning. Observe your body, behaviour, words and tone when you are getting your child to do an activity or a worksheet. Our children see a different side of us when we are making them do work. Do you think the child is enjoying the process of learning? Remember, when there is stress, learning is not as effective.

I have seen how my own anxiety comes in the way of my child learning to read. Saiveer had earlier enjoyed learning letter sounds and blending sounds to make words, but suddenly, I found that he did not want to read anymore. Every time I would tell him to read, he would run away or not show any interest. When I reflected on the situation, I realized that I was getting impatient with his progress and correcting him more than was required. Because I really wanted him to read, I was putting a lot of pressure on myself and in turn transferring it to him. When Saiveer started to read, I observed that my body started getting strained as I grew anxious wanting him to read well.

When I realized this, I started to pay attention to my breathing and tried to consciously keep my body calm during the time he read. I also affirmed to myself that my child is learning at his own pace and to become more patient. I knew that with patience,

I could overcome the situation and make Saiveer fall in love with reading. On the other hand, it was clear that my impatience was creating problems and taking me away from my goal.

A consistent change in my attitude and behaviour around Saiveer's reading helped me reinstate my child's interest in the activity.

When we stay patient and calm, we are able to maintain our connection with our children, which we need to get them to cooperate in their studies. Remember, our children are going to study for many years. It is important to look at the long-term perspective and aim to create a positive association with academics, because that can make things smoother in the future, making our children more independent and responsible for their work. When we focus only on the short-term goal of getting that day's work done by getting angry or threatening the child, we increase our future struggles around their studies.

2. *Make the process of studying more positive:* As discussed in the last point, a positive association is a basic requirement to help children study better. Let us see what we can do while being calm to make studies more positive, fun and stress-free for our children:

   a. Give fewer instructions and correct less. Children will not do everything perfectly; after all, they are learning. Thus, we need to be more tolerant when our children are doing their work. Avoid using words like 'You are doing the work too slowly', 'You are not forming the letters nicely' or 'You are making too many mistakes'. These remarks demotivate children and suck all the fun out of the learning process. If you do need to encourage them to do better, focus on what they are doing right more than their mistakes.

For example, use sentences such as 'You focused so well with this letter, it came out nice', and 'You are getting better at this concept now, I can see the change'. And if you do want to correct them, be more positive in your words, 'You can do it better than this', 'You don't feel like writing neatly today, is it?' or 'I think you need to say "I can do it" three times and then continue to get more energy for the work'.

b. Laugh with them and make the process fun: Find moments to connect by laughing and enjoying. For example, when Saiveer would write and the formation of the letters was off, I would say things like 'This letter's head is getting hurt as it is going out of the lines. This letter's feet got hurt, let's make it better'. And both of us would laugh. We can find innovative ways of working with our children when we are more patient.

There may be times when our child wants to tell us something right in the middle of their work. In most such situations we tell them, 'Not now, later, first do your work'. But if we listen to them and take interest for just thirty to sixty seconds before we stop them, it makes them feel heard and helps them focus better for the rest of the time spent studying. For example, if they start telling you something about what happened in school with a friend, listen for thirty seconds and say, 'Oh really, that sounds funny. Now let us complete this so that I can listen to the whole story.'

We can also make the process of learning fun by going beyond the conventional pen-and-paper method and introducing play-based learning. Many children, especially in the early years, learn much better when they manipulate objects and are practically involved in understanding a new concept. For example, when learning to add numbers, instead of counting on their fingers, we can practise with real objects.

I remember that as my son loved to colour, I would make him colour a box at the end of each sentence while practising reading sentences with him. It was a small addition to the activity, but it effectively increased his interest and cooperation in doing the task. There are so many ways we can make studies more fun and exciting for our children. There are numerous ideas parents can look up online as well.

3. *Keep expectations realistic:* One of the reasons why studies become stressful is that we start expecting

more from our child than they are capable of doing. All children, even those in the same class, have different capabilities. For instance, when children join school at the age of three and a half and are introduced to writing, some may not yet be ready to hold the pencil and write letters in the book as their fine motor skills are still developing. They may be ready within a few months, but if we start pressuring the child to write like other children, it leads to a lot of stress around learning the skill to write. This can make the child lose interest in writing completely or even going to school sometimes, resulting in long-term struggles.

The solution to this is to understand our children's pace of learning and their unique capabilities and interests instead of comparing them with other children or expecting them to perform beyond their aptitude. Sometimes parents also think, 'My child can do better than this, but does not focus enough' or 'My child can score so well, but does not seem interested to do so.' Here, firstly remember that we need our children to ultimately become self-motivated instead of studying and performing for us. Help them see that they can do better, but do not make them feel bad for their performance. Getting angry and pushing them to do more may make them demotivated or anxious about studying, taking us further away instead of closer to our goal. Take my example: Saiveer struggles to write neatly and I know that if he focuses, he can write much better. But if I start comparing his writing with that of other children and get impatient, telling him repeatedly to 'write nicely', he may stop wanting to write altogether and that will start a whole new struggle for me. So, instead, I ask him, 'Do you like the way you have written? If you do, then I am also okay with it.' This helps him find self-motivation and when I do not push him, he erases the letters he has formed and tries writing them again. Also, in the process, he learns patience and perseverance. So, it is imperative that we parents increase our tolerance to increase our children's interest in learning.

4. *Children should feel that they can do the work:* We can manage this by making the everyday goal of studying achievable. If a child struggles in completing the given task each day, feeling like it is a punishment, it is difficult for them to be motivated the next day to come back to the same practice or work. No wonder then that the minute we tell our children to study, we face opposition. Understanding our child's ability and keeping it realistic, being more patient and making study time fun, and letting children feel that they are capable of completing the given task without too much stress attached, help them form better long-term associations with learning.

For example, if we are struggling with our five-year-old to do five pages of work in a day, we can reduce the work to two pages, or if they struggle to read ten lines in one go, we can bring it down to four lines. The goal is to let them know that they can do it. We can say after they complete the task, 'Wow you completed it, high five, now let's play' to help them feel good about themselves. We can keep increasing the complexity and length of the task as the days pass, forming a better association with study time.

5. *Anticipate some kind of struggle at times:* We know studying can be boring. Children are still building their focus, will and perseverance. Thus, there are bound to be times when they will say, 'I don't want to do it'. Instead of getting irritated, it is better that we validate this feeling and also set the boundary: 'I know it gets boring sometimes. But we still have to do it.' We can use the 'bug theory' I discussed in Section 5 to help children with their willpower or we can use consequences a few times.

Our ultimate goal is not for our children to learn only what we are teaching that particular day, week, month or year—we want our children to become lifelong learners. Some days will obviously be better than others when it comes to making our children study, but our patience on the more difficult days will take us forward to our long-term goal for our children. When children fall in love with the process of learning, they will keep imbibing lessons on new things in life, which is a necessary skill to succeed in a world which is advancing and changing at such a fast pace.

18

Joint Families

Raising children in joint families has its advantages as well as challenges for parents. Living in a country like India, where many children are growing up within larger family dynamics (including my own), I decided to include this chapter in my book. I receive a lot of concerns from parents living in joint families and most of these tend to revolve around:

- boundaries not being followed due to other members' interference
- not everyone follows the same parenting style and
- parents lose connection with their children because they end up making all the rules while other family members pamper the child.

Here are some insights that may help you in dealing with these challenges:

1. Focus on what you can control as parents and work on that instead of fixating on things that you do not have control over.

Living in joint families, where grandparents, uncles, aunts and other children are living under the same roof, may throw up many situations that might be beyond our control and may interfere with the boundaries we want to set for our kids in terms of screen time, eating habits and behaviour that they are learning from different people. Parents often complain:

'My child gets the screen from his grandparents.'
'My child eats junk with the older siblings.'
'My child is learning bad words from their uncle.'

While these concerns are valid, we must remember one thing as the bottom line, 'We cannot change what we cannot control.'

There may be a lot of things that we are not able to control in larger families, but there are also many things that we can. For example, we can control the boundaries in the room when we are alone with our children; we can regulate our own behaviour; we can maintain our own connection with our children; we can form a routine for our children that is more convenient for us and so on. But, when we constantly focus on what others are doing, we lose focus on what we ourselves are doing and what we can do in order to make things easier.

Let me share my example: Saiveer's grandfather would offer him chocolate after coming back from work. This timing coincided with my son's dinner time and having the chocolate would make Saiveer lose his appetite. This situation bothered me a lot, but the fact was that I could not really control it.

So, I sat back and thought about what I could do to control this situation. I realized that I controlled what time my son would have dinner. I decided to bring forward Saiveer's dinner time by twenty minutes and made sure that he finished his meal before his grandfather came home. This effectively made the chocolate an after-dinner treat for Saiveer.

One more option here was to talk to Saiveer's grandfather about the situation. What would have been important in that case would be the manner in which that conversation would be conducted. I will discuss this in the next few points.

In another example, a client of mine was concerned that her daughter was watching television with her grandmother in the afternoon in spite of having her own screen time in the morning. This considerably increased the amount of time her daughter spent on screens. So we brainstormed about all the possibilities that were under the client's control and came up with the idea that she could do away with her daughter's morning screen time and shift it entirely to the afternoon. My client also realized that she could take her own me-time during this afternoon screen time, which would help revive her own energy for some quality time with her child later in the evening.

Apart from this, there were other possible solutions in this scenario. For example, my client could have scheduled a class for the daughter in the afternoon or spent time playing with her daughter so that the child did not get involved in watching TV. We simply have to figure out what we can control and work around it to find ways to deal with a situation.

Let me emphasize here that I am not defending other family members in any way; I am just trying to empower parents by helping them shift their focus to what they can control, instead of only complaining about what they cannot. This helps us direct our energy towards things that we can manipulate and effectively change situations in our favour.

2. Work on your connection with your child

One of the things that we can control and work on is building a connection with our child. We have talked a lot about connection in the book. When we work on the quality of interaction we have with our children, when we are careful not to put our frustrations on our kids, when we maintain respect towards our little ones, and when we accept their nature and love them as they are, we can maintain a strong connection with them in spite of the rules and boundaries that we create for them.

There may be times when we feel that our child is getting influenced by another family member and picking up their habits or spending more time with them. In such situations, it is important that we do not take it personally but give respect to our child's relationships with others. We have to remind ourselves that our children are forming a unique connection with each person in the family. Also, if we get too irritated, we may get disconnected from our child, which may only end up increasing the gap between us. When we invest in our own connection, we automatically become secure about our relationship with our child and thus, have increased influence over them.

3. In moments when things do not work out as planned, instead of reacting, focus on the long term.

Living in families with more family members, there will be times when things will not go as we have planned. For example, my husband and I made a rule that there would be no screen time for Saiveer before he finished his homework, but one day, we found our child watching videos on another family member's phone without completing his schoolwork. This could have made us feel really irritated and also helpless, which may have brought out a negative reaction from us towards our child. We could have asked Saiveer, 'Why are you watching the screen when we have decided you should not? This is not right!' or we may have argued with the family member in front of the child. But all this would have caused a disconnect with our child and also the family members.

When we make things into an issue in such situations, we end up creating more trouble for ourselves in the future. First, we may lose the support of the family member and second, the child may end up repeating the unwanted behaviour as they think they can easily get away with it.

So, instead of getting irritated, I approached the situation in the following way:

Before anything else, I breathed to regulate my emotions and then said to Saiveer, 'Oh you got to watch some videos with Aunty. So glad you are enjoying it. Let's give back the screen in another five minutes and then do our work so that we can enjoy some more of it later.'

In a similar situation, another may not agree with this plan. Then the parent can say, 'Okay, it seems you are not able to stop right now, so you can watch now and we can cancel the evening show we were supposed to watch. That is also fine, you can choose, sweetheart.' Even while saying all this, we must remain respectful and connected; there should be no anger accompanying these words. If the child does not want to miss the show time with us, they will themselves give up the screen that instant. This also depends on whether the child enjoys their regular show time with us and also if they believe our words, that we mean what we say. Later, when the child is not around, we can talk to the family members about the rule and gain their future cooperation.

Our focus on what we can control helps us in dealing with our situations in smarter ways instead of letting our emotions come in our way and making us react in unhelpful ways.

Here, I want to revisit the situation I discussed earlier involving my son and his grandfather. In an instance where Saiveer got chocolate from his grandfather before having his dinner on any day, instead of cribbing in front of my child, I choose to celebrate it with him and say, 'Wow you got chocolate from your grandfather. Yummy! I also want a bite, may I?' I did this because if my child is already eating the chocolate, I cannot do much about it, but I can at least reinforce my connection with my son and create a positive association for the next time.

If my son has not started eating the chocolate yet, I say, 'Wow, you got a chocolate! Let's keep it in the pocket safely so that we can enjoy it after we finish our meal. Where is your pocket?' But I make sure to express happiness for his treat because it is very difficult for children to feel connected to us if they feel that what makes them happy makes us unhappy.

4. Remember your child is watching how tolerant you are

What do we want our children to do when things do not go according to what they want? For example, they want to play more video games but they can't, the teacher gets upset with them in school or they have to go to a class that do not want to attend. Don't we want them to be more understanding and more tolerant? We want them to understand that sometimes, things may not happen the way we wish them to, and that is a fact of life.

Now, if we observe ourselves, how do we behave when things go against our wishes in the family? How do we react when other people behave in ways we do not like? Do we get too irritated and start complaining or do we breathe and let things pass and approach the situation with a calm mind? Do we crib and complain or do we adjust and move on? What is our level of tolerance?

Our children are observing these things, especially when we live in larger families. If we see our children complaining a lot, then we need to be vigilant about whether we are doing the same in our personal situations while our children are around us. Remember, to raise children with better resilience, we need to model that in front of them.

5. Collaborate instead of blame

There are a lot of ways in which we can approach other family members to share our concerns about our children. For example, if we are worried about our child consuming bad-quality screen time, eating too much junk food or falling sick frequently, we need the cooperation of the other family members to deal with those situations effectively.

In such situations, how we talk to the other family members matters a great deal. We can either say, 'My son is eating too much junk food in your room. It is making him fall sick or it is not good for him.' Or we can begin with, 'I was wondering if his eating habits are the reason for his low immunity. Do you think we can do something about it? How can we help him?'

The former sounds like an accusation, like you are blaming them because of the words or tone being used. The latter puts forward our concern for the child while making the other person feel that they are in the same team with us, wanting the best for the child. After all, the other family members also love the child, and when we keep the well-being of the child at the centre of the discussion and are conscious of the way we talk, it makes a lot of difference in how they receive our message and how much they cooperate with us.

6. The child is learning how different people behave differently in various situations

Every person in the family may have a different way of dealing with children. Some may be too pampering, some may be too strict and some may not take as much interest in interacting with kids. Parents often worry about how another family member is not following the parenting style that they are following and how that will affect their child. This is especially the case when the parent is trying to shift towards gentle or conscious parenting.

If we think about it, living in a joint family presents an opportunity for children to learn about human behaviour. If everyone starts behaving and responding in the same way, how will a child learn that different people behave differently in different situations? In a way, it is good for the child that everyone has their own way of dealing with them. It also helps them build more resilience. Thus, till the time it is not detrimental, we need to let our children experience interacting with different personalities in the house and learn to build their own relationships with each family member.

7. Respect your child if you want other family members to do the same

The way we behave with our children in front of other family members sets a pattern for other family members to follow. If we often get angry with our child, other family members are likely to start following the same pattern. And the same thing happens when we give respect to our children.

Sometimes I have heard parents say, 'Before someone else gets angry at my child, I myself correct my child or shout at him. Because I do not want someone else to shout at my child.' But this is counterproductive because when we do that:

- we are letting other people know that it is okay to shout at our child
- we are disconnecting ourselves from our child and helping to reinforce the connection of the other member with our child and

- we are not letting the child go through the natural consequences that may teach them how other people may react to such situations.

Thus, it is important that we confidently choose our own way of dealing and behaving with our children without getting influenced by other family members.

8. A complaining mind increases problems

Every family structure has some advantages and some disadvantages. I have heard so many parents living in nuclear families say that they miss having more family members around them, who can share some household responsibilities and look after the child sometimes so that they can step out, etc.

To be happier, it is essential that we start looking at the advantages of living in joint families much more than thinking about the challenges that we face. We will be surprised to see how just a change in our mindset can start making situations easier for us in the family. A complaining mindset increases problems for us while a positive mindset has the power to not only solve our situations but increase our quality of life in many ways by attracting love and abundance for us and our children.

Conclusion

*'We are not aiming to be perfect parents or to have
perfect children—
we are aiming for a genuine human relationship
with our children,
where we accept them for who they are and help
them reach their true potential,
where we learn to love and accept ourselves and
evolve in the process,
where we are empowered because we are more
informed,
where we are more present for our children
because we are more conscious!'*

At the end of the book, I want to remind my readers that
as parents, you have the best capacity to understand
your children and just need the right knowledge and
tools to aid you in the process. With the information
provided in this book, I hope to take you closer to truly

connecting with your children, feeling more empowered and reaching your own parenting goals better.

You have just encountered a lot of information in this book; it may make sense to you and you may even relate to it, but know that in reality, it is not possible to apply everything suggested here all at once. In order to bring in real transformation in your relationship with your child, you must begin by learning to be patient with yourself. We parents need to start by pausing, observing and reflecting before we can even begin to make changes. We will make mistakes along the way, as mistakes are a part of growing and learning, and not let them make us feel terrible or guilty. However, learning to embrace these mistakes and picking up the lessons from them are the first steps towards bringing authentic change.

Change will surely come—first because you can now finally see your own behaviour in a different light and know that there are better ways to regulate yourselves. Second, feeling all your emotions and letting them pass without judging yourself is an important part of the process of healing yourself and breaking old unhelpful patterns. Armed with more self-awareness and new helpful tools, I hope you will begin to make beautiful changes in your parenting journey.

At the beginning of your gentle parenting journey, you may find that you are still continuing with your old patterns of behaviour and automatic responses which you have been used to for so many years until this point. I remember that even armed with the knowledge I had about children—from my educational background—after becoming a parent, it took me quite a bit of time to come out of my own conditioning, traumas and patterns to become the kind of parent I really wanted to be. I believe I am still learning and evolving every day.

We need to remember that knowing is the first step towards transformation, and then comes applying and internalizing the knowledge. Thus, we need to learn to forgive ourselves as well as love and accept ourselves in the process of becoming better parents. When I started working on being calm, there were so many times I would lose it and then feel extremely guilty about it. But whenever I was too hard on myself, I made more mistakes instead of getting better. I learnt then, that to bring about true transformation, it is important that I am more patient with myself and accept myself. This helped me in being patient with and accepting my child as well. Parenting is a journey of learning and unlearning, in which we are raising ourselves at the same time as raising these little beings.

There is no parent who does not face challenges with their children at different ages and stages. It is time we decide what kind of parents we want to be: We can either be parents who stress out and start complaining whenever situations become difficult or we can be parents who practise being calm and find better ways to deal with the situations. So, ask yourself, 'How do I want to face these challenges?' A small change in our perspective and thoughts can bring about tremendous change in our actions and thus, in our lives.

Before I end this book, I do want to reinforce a few points that we have discussed in greater detail throughout the book:

1. **Make connection your priority:** When we work on strengthening our connection with our children, it gets easier dealing with a lot of challenges. As we discussed, connection gives us more influence over our children's behaviour and the decisions they make. Losing this influence can cause a lot of distress for us because ultimately, we can't control what our children will do.

   Whenever you feel lost during a phase in your parenting, before applying any techniques or strategies, work on your connection with your children. No strategy can work effectively if there is a disconnection in the relationship. In fact, most often, that is the missing piece which causes the struggle. Having a strong parent–child connection makes other parenting strategies even more effective.

   And remember, we may feel very connected to our child at some times and not so much at other times—this is completely normal. What is important is that we prioritize maintaining our connection and keep falling back on it because it is a long-term investment that is sure to lead to amazing benefits.

2. **Get to the underlying cause of your child's behaviour before judging them:** Whenever you feel,

'How can my child behave like this?' or 'Why is my child doing this?' start investigating the cause of their behaviour and think, 'Where is this behaviour coming from?' or 'What can be underlying this behaviour?' There is *always* some reason that prompts our children's behaviour. A small change in our thought process can make us calmer and kinder and thus, more helpful as a parent in any situation. One question that I always ask my son when he is acting up is, 'Saiveer, are you not feeling good?' before I comment on and discipline the behaviour. It is important that we connect with the underlying feelings so that we can effectively change the behaviour.

3. **Reflect on your own behaviour:** Always keep in mind, your behaviour tremendously affects your children's behaviour. So, whenever we see increased tantrums, defiance and stubbornness in our child, it is important to first ask ourselves, 'What is my behaviour and state of mind like when I am around my child?' Our impatience, irritation, stress and disconnection influence our children's behaviour and I cannot stress this point enough. And remember what 'being calm' actually looks like. It is not only that we are not showing anger when we are calm— having a calm body and a calm mind is important to see the true results of calm parenting.

4. **Understand children and be realistic:** By now, we have understood that our children's brains are very different from adult brains. So, it is essential that we

have realistic expectations of them. This helps us maintain a calm approach towards them and thus, connect with them better. Also, being realistic with our children means being realistic with ourselves as parents as it helps us see our children's behaviours as part of their development instead of taking them personally.

Understanding our children, their true nature and uniqueness, and accepting them as they are instead of comparing them, are important steps in becoming conscious parents. This not only helps us in having a positive relationship with our children but also helps our children develop confidence and self-esteem, which are the building blocks of success.

5. **Allow children to feel feelings:** Children lack the capacity for emotional regulation; thus, where there are children, there will be drama. Instead of being scared of our children's tantrums, we must learn to deal with them calmly, and in fact, see them as opportunities. Children need to experience all kinds of emotions as they grow as that helps them become emotionally resilient, provided we parents play our part right. We can do this by:

- validating and empathizing, and not judging our children;
- regulating our own emotions, modelling better ways of behaving, and not throwing our own tantrums

- talking about their emotions later and helping them reflect on the experience, and
- talking about our own emotions openly as much as possible without burdening them.

These steps will help us in building a strong foundation for children's emotional intelligence.

6. **An important mantra to remember is 'I can only do what I can and that's it':** If we think about it, in any situation with our children, we only have a few options of behaviours to choose from. For example, when a child throws a tantrum in a public place, what can we do? We can either pick the child up and take them to a corner, we can start shouting at our child or we can ignore our child. There is not much else we can do except choose from the options available in a situation. But when we calm ourselves down, we are able to see our options clearly and choose the one that is the most helpful for us, instead of making a choice that worsens the situation.

Thus, my last message to you all is that whenever you feel stuck as a parent, no matter how difficult the situation is, instead of stressing out, remember this mantra: **'I can only do what I can and that's it.'** Then do your best by calming yourself and remembering what you control, leaving the rest. Know that each challenge that we face does not last but comes and goes. It is how we handle the challenge and what we learn from the experience that matters the most. After all, parenting is as fulfilling as it is challenging, and all parents experience both in their journey—no one is perfect.

Notes

Chapter 4: Aligning Our Expectations to How Our Children's Brains Work

1 Daniel Siegel and Tina Payne Bryson, *The Whole Brain Child* (New York: Bantam Books, 2012).

Chapter 6: How Can We Build a Connection with Our Children?

1 Kyle Benson, 'The Magic Relationship Ratio, According to Science', Gottman Institute, 8 August 2022, https://www.gottman.com/blog/the-magic-relationship-ratio-according-science/.

Chapter 9: What Is Stopping Us from Being Calm Parents?

1 Aaron T. Beck, Cognitive Behavioural Therapy (New York: Guilford Press, 2020).

2   Rhonda Byrne, *The Secret* (New York: Atria Books, 2006).

3. Louise Hay, *You Can Heal Your Life* (California: Hay House Inc., 1984).

Chapter 12: Common Ways of Disciplining Children and Why They Don't Work

1   Daniel J. Siegel and Tina Payne Bryson, *No-Drama Discipline: The Whole-Brain Way to Calm the Chaos and Nurture Your Child's Developing Mind* (New York: Bantam, 2014).

Scan QR code to access the
Penguin Random House India website